Vocabulary Workout for the SAT/ACT

Volume 3

Vocabulary Workout for the SAT/ACT

Volume 3

Justin Grosslight

Published by JJMG Enterprises LLC

Editorial:
Justin Grosslight, head author and editor.

ISBN: 978-0-9984841-3-6

10 9 8 7 6 5 4 3 2 1

Preface

Becoming an expert in any language is hard work. Regardless of whether English is your mother tongue, more advanced reading and vocabulary skills often accrue slowly and only with a sustained commitment. Because of this, transitioning from communicating in popular English to becoming a consumer of scholarly and intellectual prose can be an arduous journey. While there is no supplement for reading erudite materials, building a vocabulary and an understanding of intellectual concepts is critical for language mastery.

In writing the *Vocabulary Workout* series, I had in mind the myriad individuals who are fluent in conversational English but who want to take their writing skills and vocabulary to the next level. Many of today's students and professionals seek to build these skills, but find the task extraneous to their immediate needs, overly pedantic, or dreadfully time consuming. The *Vocabulary Workout* series aims to ease that process. Unlike other vocabulary books, many of which are merely extended lists, ours are replete with exercises; there are also lessons to help you understand the roots of words and intellectual terms. And the words are useful: they have been gleaned from statistical examination of dozens of SAT® and ACT® college entrance exams, which in turn excerpt their readings from a wide array of sophisticated prose materials.

This is the third volume in a four-volume series. A complete edition that combines all four of volumes of this series is also available. The words in these books are suitable for either classroom study or independent preparation. Do note, however, that these words do not constitute an exhaustive vocabulary list necessary for success.

Writing these books has been an evolving process, and I have enjoyed receiving feedback as it develops. In particular, I would like to thank Vu Le, Antonio Madrid, Uyen Nguyen, and especially Yannick Lalonde for their contributions, sustained support, and constructive criticism. Several students – Helen Dang, Duc Doan, Julian Ho, Quoc Huynh, Phong Le, Alice Nguyen, Nguyen Nguyen, and Hannah Truong – have gladly provided input and frank suggestions as they used drafts of this book to prepare for their SAT® examinations. I also would like to thank Dr. Clive Keevil for allowing pilot versions of these lessons to be taught at the Australian International School (AIS) in Ho Chi Minh City. Last but not least, I would like to thank Robert Fouldes and Huong Nguyen for their cover design upon the book's completion.

I hope that this book will be as immensely useful to you as it has been for the students who used it in its gestation period. With that said, good luck on your vocabulary endeavors!

Justin Grosslight

How to Use This Book

As was the case in our previous two volumes, this book is intended to help build your vocabulary; it is a strategically organized catalogue of 250 words that appear in intellectual and scholarly English, especially in college and university entrance examinations. It is not, however, intended to be your sole source of learning words. Ideally, this book should be used in tandem with reading other scholarly and intellectual materials to help nurture your vocabulary growth.

Often to fully understand a word and its meaning(s), it is helpful to see a word used in context many times. To reinforce this idea, the exercises contained in this book often require dictionary use. By looking up words in a dictionary, you can read samples of their uses in various settings and then apply what you have learned to the exercises in this text. Doing so will provide an active approach to building an extensive vocabulary. This book's exercises also use a consistent intellectual vocabulary to complement the focal words of each lesson. Learning these words should further enhance your verbal skills.

At a stable pace, one should be able to absorb approximately fifty words, or ten lessons, per week. We have provided review quizzes after every ten lessons to help facilitate your study. One can study more words, of course, but diminishing returns may occur if more than twenty lessons are absorbed each week. Ideally this book should be studied at a moderate pace consistently over a long duration, allowing for time to let words sink in slowly. There are also many reasons why someone should use this book: whether you want to build a more solid vocabulary, you want to prepare for an examination, or you simply hope to sound erudite, all are good reasons for using this text. Whatever your purpose of study, however, it is imperative that you never cease to explore new vocabularies.

Possessing a solid vocabulary can help you enter a strong academic program, can make you more attractive for a corporate job, and can make you sound more articulate and knowledgeable. I hope you enjoy the third leg of your quest to broaden your vocabulary with this book.

TABLE OF CONTENTS

NEW WORDS

rudimentary
ˌro͞odəˈment(ə)rē

winnow
ˈwinō

elicit
iˈlisit

perturbed
pərˈtərbd

multifaceted
ˌməltiˈfasətəd, ˌməltī-

Lesson 121

A SIMPLE SOLUTION

The viral, **multifaceted** disease appeared so suddenly that even the brightest minds around the world were **perturbed** by its sudden outbreak. Copious amounts of research were carried out, yet no treatments could be identified. After months of **winnowing** a mass of research papers, Annie finally came to the surprising conclusion that a **rudimentary** approach was the best way to end this blight. She was able to **elicit** a response from the virus by injecting a stimulating enzyme commonly found in abundance in the tropics. Annie became internationally recognized for her contribution.

Definitions: Try matching the words in the list with the appropriate definitions. If you are stuck, check the glossary in the back of the book or the passage at the top of the page.

1.	rudimentary	_____	a.	to distinguish; to sift out; to separate out
2.	winnow	_____	b.	basic; elementary
3.	elicit	_____	c.	troubled; perplexed
4.	perturbed	_____	d.	versatile; having many aspects
5.	multifaceted	_____	e.	to evoke; to draw out

Sentences: Try to use the words above in a sentence below. Remember that a word ending may be changed or its figure of speech slightly altered.

6.   James was extremely _____ by his boss' enigmatic statement regarding his future employment.

7.   It is a detective's primary objective to _____ the list of possible suspects in a crime down to one likely culprit.

8.   The first step in dealing with a recession is releasing a(n) _____ Stimulus Package that bolsters many aspects of the economy simultaneously.

9.   The contraption may appear to be _____ in design, but it is extremely effective in mitigating the impacts of pollution.

10.   The movie *Interstellar* (2014) _____ a sense of existential crisis in many of its viewers.

1

Lesson 122

POETIC JUSTICE

During the **inception** of his restaurant, Ming was a sedulous man, working over ten hours a day and never **procrastinating** on any tasks because he wanted to bathe in opulence. Despite his efforts, business **waxed** and waned for many years. Ming became desperate that his business was not steadily growing and started to **desecrate** the ethics of his competition by demeaning other restaurants on the Internet. His actions led to a huge influx of customers, making him extremely happy. Yet despite having loads of new, **cloying** customers, Ming realized that if he continued to use strong spices in recipes, people would stop frequenting his restaurant.

NEW WORDS

desecration
ˌdesiˈkrāSHən

procrastinate
prəˈkrastəˌnāt, prō-

wax
waks

inception
inˈsepSHən

cloying
kloing

Definitions: Try matching the words in the list with the appropriate definitions. If you are stuck, check the glossary in the back of the book or the passage at the top of the page.

1.	desecration	_____	a.	to delay or put off
2.	procrastinate	_____	b.	to become larger
3.	wax	_____	c.	displeasing because of excess of sweetness or richness or sentiment
4.	inception	_____	d.	blasphemy; violation
5.	cloying	_____	e.	beginning; initiation

Sentences: Try to use the words above in a sentence below. Remember that a word ending may be changed or its figure of speech slightly altered.

6. We know the moon is _____ when the light part grows larger with the passing days, indicating that it is shifting toward a full moon.

7. The act of demolishing historical sites to make way for high-rise office buildings is a _____ of the country's cultural heritage.

8. The _____ of the Internet marked the beginning of contemporary globalization.

9. One of the reasons why most people found *The Twilight Saga* repulsive is because of its _____ romance.

10. It is much preferable to accomplish a given task immediately instead of _____ because the longer you put it off, the harder it is to begin.

NEW WORDS

dumbfounded
ˈdəmˌfoundid

prune
pro͞on

dither
ˈdiT͟Hər

vicarious
vīˈkerēəs, vi-

reclusive
riˈklo͞osiv, -ziv

SHATTERED DREAMS

Alexa's parents were **dumbfounded** when they heard that she had not been studying for her college entrance exams. They thought that, because she had become **reclusive**, she must have been hard at work preparing for college; instead, however, she had been sitting in her room **dithering** over which boy she hoped would ask her to prom. How tragic it was for Alexa's parents to discover this, as they had hoped she would be admitted to a prestigious university and that they could **vicariously** experience life at an elite school through her stories. Alas, rather than getting into a stellar collage, Alexa created a landscaping business where she earned her salary by **pruning** trees in the gardens surrounding famous buildings.

Definitions: Try matching the words in the list with the appropriate definitions. If you are stuck, check the glossary in the back of the book or the passage at the top of the page.

1. dumbfounded _____ a. (n.) a plum preserved by drying out; (v.) to trim; to remove the superfluous elements
2. prune _____ b. experienced in the imagination through the actions or feelings of another individual
3. dither _____ c. to be indecisive
4. vicarious _____ d. unsociable; solitary
5. reclusive _____ e. astounded; bewildered

Sentences: Try to use the words above in a sentence below. Remember that a word ending may be changed or its figure of speech slightly altered.

6. It is a fallacy to consider someone _____ just because they're always at home on the computer: there's a whole social world on the Internet.
7. The senator was _____ about during the debate: he did not know what stand to take on income inequality issues.
8. Vietnamese people love to take _____ pride in their peers' accomplishments despite having played no part in the process.
9. Tim was _____ when he found out that his invention – created as a hobby – had become a worldwide phenomenon.
10. In a business environment, reports are to be _____ and kept succinct before submission.

Lesson 124

JUDGMENT LAPSE

Daisy was a really compassionate girl. Because of that, becoming the freshman representative in student congress was a perfectly **viable** option next year; in fact, it was even expected of her. However, upon entering high school, Daisy became obsessed with **enhancing** her intimidating personality, believing that this was her key to gaining popularity. She would make **sarcastic**, and sometimes toxic, remarks to everyone around her. This **miscalculation** led to her being identified by most of her peers as a **delinquent**, destroying the innocent image she once had.

Definitions: Try matching the words in the list with the appropriate definitions. If you are stuck, check the glossary in the back of the book or the passage at the top of the page.

1.	sarcastic	_____	a.	(adj.) 1. showing a tendency to commit a crime, especially youth; 2. irresponsible; 3. in arrears; (n.) a youth likely to commit a crime
2.	delinquent	_____	b.	applicable; feasible
3.	enhance	_____	c.	1. to assess a situation wrongly; 2. to measure an amount, distance, or value wrongly
4.	miscalculate	_____	d.	using irony in speech in order to mock or to show contempt
5.	viable	_____	e.	to intensify, increase, or improve the extent, quality, or value thereof

Sentences: Try to use the words above in a sentence below. Remember that a word ending may be changed or its figure of speech slightly altered.

6.   Being considered a juvenile _____ can really affect one's future.

7.   The snide remarks and _____ tone in the face of the homeless' sufferings suggest a sociopathic inability to feel empathy.

8.   While conceding is always a(n) _____ option, those who persist will be met with great rewards.

9.   A tiny engineering _____ may make an entire bridge collapse.

10.   Not only is it unscrupulous to _____ one's ability with illegal drugs, it is also punishable as a federal offense.

NEW WORDS

detonate
ˈdetnˌāt

lighthearted
ˈlītˌhärtid

pithy
ˈpiTHē

wane
wān

expropriate
ˌeksˈprōprēˌāt

Lesson 125

RUSSIA, CHINA, AGGRESSION

After repeated attempts from powers in Moscow to **detonate** a bomb in Beijing, the Chinese army threatened to **expropriate** all weapons of mass destruction from Russia. In a **pithy** statement, China's leader said, "We will take all weapons from Russia as revenge. This will cause Russia's aggression toward our nation to **wane**." Though the message was grave, the response from Russian authorities was rather **lighthearted**: they simply laughed at the Chinese show of verbal force, unaffected by any threats coming from their neighboring country.

Definitions: Try matching the words in the list with the appropriate definitions. If you are stuck, check the glossary in the back of the book or the passage at the top of the page.

1.	detonate	_____	a.	carefree; jovial
2.	lighthearted	_____	b.	to diminish or lessen
3.	pithy	_____	c.	to explode; to burst
4.	wane	_____	d.	(usually of a government) to seize and take away (usually property) from its owner
5.	expropriate	_____	e.	concise and strongly expressive

Sentences: Try to use the words above in a sentence below. Remember that a word ending may be changed or its figure of speech slightly altered.

6.   Unfortunately, the impact of China's 2014 stimulus package _____ quicker than anticipated.

7.   Under communistic regimes, citizens often have their land and resources _____ by the government in the name of the greater good.

8.   After _____ two homemade pressure cooker bombs during the Boston Marathon, the culprits attempted to escape but were quickly identified and arrested.

9.   A good businessperson is able to give _____ statements summarizing his or her business plans.

10.   The story's _____ beginning quickly devolved into a dark, gritty theme.

Lesson 126

DRINKING PROBLEM

Unfortunately, the city of Harbor Ridge has had an environmental problem that has **menaced** its fresh water reserves. For the past two years, a corporate chemical plant has been dumping its waste into the nearby river, which has made local water no longer **potable**. The city has hired environmental experts to **apprise** them of the gravity of the problem, and also lawyers to inform municipal officials whether the corporate behavior poisoning the drinking water is **illicit**. Chances are high that the city will take action, but surely there will be a **divergence** of views between city representatives and corporate management. Hopefully a solution can be found that will benefit all parties.

Definitions: Try matching the words in the list with the appropriate definitions. If you are stuck, check the glossary in the back of the book or the passage at the top of the page.

1.	apprise	_____	a.	(n.) 1. a danger or threat; 2. a person or thing causing a danger or threat; (v.) to threaten in a hostile manner
2.	menace	_____	b.	to inform or advise
3.	illicit	_____	c.	something safe to drink; drinkable
4.	diverge	_____	d.	illegal; prohibited
5.	potable	_____	e.	to separate from a path or route and go in a different direction

Sentences: Try to use the words above in a sentence below. Remember that a word ending may be changed or its figure of speech slightly altered.

6. Humans are sometimes considered as a(n) _____ to the Earth because they are polluting it with their waste.

7. Politicians can tend to _____ from the main topic of discussion to reinforce their own agenda, especially during a debate.

8. Because the tap water in many rural areas is not _____, residents must resort to drinking bottled mineral water to stay hydrated.

9. It is a lawyer's job to _____ his or her clients of the best course of action in a legal quagmire.

10. In order to obtain the necessary evidence to stop any large-scale _____ activities, the national security bodies need to send undercover agents.

NEW WORDS

foible
ˈfoibəl

reparation
ˌrepəˈrāSHən

venerate
ˈvenəˌrāt

equivocate
iˈkwivəˌkāt

ingenious
inˈjēnyəs

Lesson 127

MYSTERIOUS GENIUS

Mark is **venerated** for his **ingenuity** in the field of robotics. He is able to **repair** androids of great intricacy while many of his colleagues fail to understand their basic structure. However, one of his personal **foibles** was that he does not like to share his knowledge. He always **equivocates** when probed about his methods for repairing robots. Mark is truly an enigmatic figure.

Definitions: Try matching the words in the list with the appropriate definitions. If you are stuck, check the glossary in the back of the book or the passage at the top of the page.

1.	foible	_____	a.	to revere; to idolize
2.	reparation	_____	b.	a minor weakness, defect, or eccentricity in someone's behavior
3.	venerate	_____	c.	to use ambiguous language to avoid commitment or to hide the truth
4.	equivocate	_____	d.	clever; brilliant
5.	ingenious	_____	e.	restitution; making amends; paying money to those who have been wronged

Sentences: Try to use the words above in a sentence below. Remember that a word ending may be changed or its figure of speech slightly altered.

6.   After a thief was caught on camera stealing $1,800 from Regina's purse at the casino, Regina sued the casino and sought _____ for lost funds.

7.   Thanks to Steve Jobs' _____ innovation, Apple was able to become one of the leading electronics corporations in the world.

8.   Many politicians _____ on issues instead of addressing problems directly.

9.   A husband should love everything about his wife, including her _____.

10.   It is fascinating that, to us, the mathematician Galileo Galilei (1564-1642) is a(n) _____ figure, though the Church considered him a social pariah when he was alive.

Lesson 128

INCONGRUENT SISTERS

It was hard to believe that Marilyn and Elizabeth were siblings, for they were totally different in character. Marilyn was extremely **demure** and always kind to those around her. Elizabeth, on the other hand, was **unadorned** with civilities and bluntly told people how she felt. Often Elizabeth would try to **spur** on a quarrel with Marilyn by telling her that she was **hypocritical** in that she never said what she actually thought. Marilyn, however, generally ignored her sister. In Marilyn's view, Elizabeth was harder to stomach than **fetid** produce. Such was the life of two very different sisters.

Definitions: Try matching the words in the list with the appropriate definitions. If you are stuck, check the glossary in the back of the book or the passage at the top of the page.

1.	hypocritical	_____	a.	plain and simple, undecorated
2.	unadorned	_____	b.	smelling extremely unpleasant
3.	fetid	_____	c.	behaving in a way that indicates someone has higher moral standards than is reality
4.	demure	_____	d.	to incite or stimulate
5.	spur	_____	e.	reserved, modest, and shy

Sentences: Try to use the words above in a sentence below. Remember that a word ending may be changed or its figure of speech slightly altered.

6.   Despite growing up as a(n) _____ girl, Isabella quickly became pompous after entering university.

7.   Sven's excessive opulence definitely served to _____ his egotistical and arrogant personality.

8.   It is _____ for a person who smokes five packs of cigarettes each day to extol the value of being cigarette free for health reasons.

9.   It is best to relay the truth in a(n) _____ and direct manner.

10.   Because Paul had not cleaned the kitchen in nearly two months, a(n) _____ scent emanated from the kitchen space.

NEW WORDS

avert
ə'vərt

benefactors
'benə‚faktər, ‚benə'faktər

impoverish
im'päv(ə)riSH

proclivity
prō'klivətē, prə-

reserve
ri'zərv

Politicians always seek strong **benefactors** to sponsor their campaign. However, these wealthy people have the **proclivity** to promote their own personal agenda, **averting** their eyes away from the real social issues. The **impoverished** continue to remain in the slums while the wealthy climb toward the sky, **reserving** a seat next to the gods overlooking the ghettos. As these opulent individuals reign supremely over the country by influencing the politicians, the status quo is maintained.

Definitions: Try matching the words in the list with the appropriate definitions. If you are stuck, check the glossary in the back of the book or the passage at the top of the page.

1.   avert   _____   a.   to prevent or ward off an undesirable occurrence
2.   benefactors   _____   b.   people who give money or other help to a person or a cause
3.   impoverish   _____   c.   avoid
4.   proclivity   _____   d.   to exhaust; to reduce to poverty
5.   reserve   _____   e.   tendency; inclination

Sentences: Try to use the words above in a sentence below. Remember that a word ending may be changed or its figure of speech slightly altered.

6.   It is extremely vital to have the correct kind of _____ for any entrepreneurial endeavors.
7.   India is one of the many places in the world where the affluent can be seen next to the _____.
8.   Tucker called the restaurant to _____ a table for three for dinner.
9.   Ulla has a(n) _____ for giving up in the face of adversity, no matter how insignificant.
10.   _____ the issue is only delaying the inevitable; people must compromise to effectively solve the problem.

9

Lesson 130

RESPECTABLE FIGURE

Harshim grew up in the slums of Mumbai, **ostracized** by other children because of his fixation with waste. He went through many periods of **malaise** during childhood, living among the trash. Harshim had only one dream, which was to one day clean the world and provide everyone with a healthy living environment. He worked **sedulously** to make his dream materialize. One day, Harshim created a **receptacle** that could automatically discern the difference between recyclable and non-recyclable rubbish. The simple machine could also sort different types of trash with a special operation that prevents **mischance** from ever occurring. His life has changed completely since then, for he has finally achieved his ultimate goal.

Definitions: Try matching the words in the list with the appropriate definitions. If you are stuck, check the glossary in the back of the book or the passage at the top of the page.

1.	sedulous	_____	a.	to exclude someone from a group
2.	ostracize	_____	b.	assiduous; diligent
3.	mischance	_____	c.	depression, anxiety
4.	receptacle	_____	d.	bad luck
5.	malaise	_____	e.	container; a place for holding or storing

Sentences: Try to use the words above in a sentence below. Remember that a word ending may be changed or its figure of speech slightly altered.

6. Marsha was _____ at the party because she wore a dress that was far too casual for the fancy event.

7. Elon Musk, the CEO of Tesla Motors and SpaceX, is often described as a(n) _____ worker because he spends over 100 hours per week performing occupational tasks.

8. It is a nice gesture to clean the bottles and remove labels before placing them in the recycling _____.

9. A crucial trait of successful entrepreneurs is their ability to overcome the _____ they often feel from experiencing continuous failures in getting a business launched.

10. There should always be auxiliary plans in case a(n) _____ occurs during the original implementation.

Crossword Puzzle
Lessons 121-130

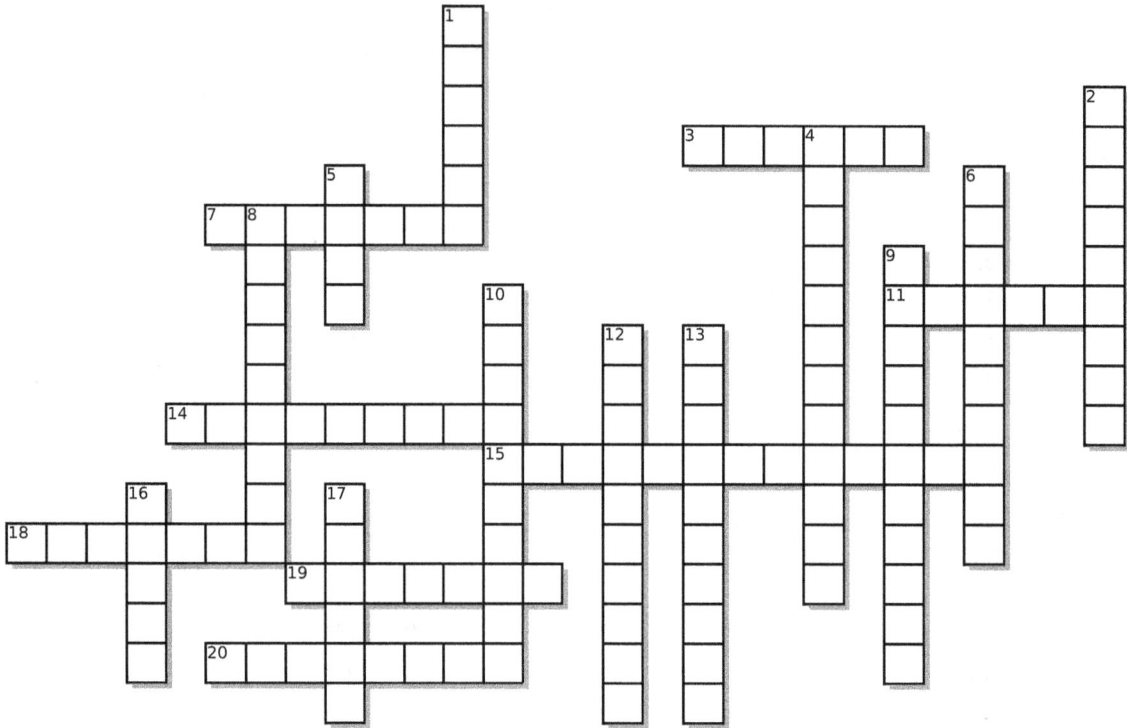

ACROSS

3 to be indecisive
7 something safe to drink; drinkable
11 to evoke; to draw out
14 unsociable; solitary
15 to delay or put off
18 to separate from a path or route and go in a different direction
19 to intensify, increase, or improve the quality, value, or extent of
20 to explode; to burst

DOWN

1 a minor weakness, defect, or eccentricity in someone's behavior
2 beginning; initiation

4 behaving in a way that indicates someone has higher moral standards than is reality
5 to diminish or lessen
6 (adj.) 1. showing a tendency to commit a crime, especially youth; 2. irresponsible; 3. in arrears; (n.) a youth likely to commit a crime
8 to exclude someone from a group
9 people who give money or other help to a person or a cause
10 container; a place for holding or storing
12 tendency; inclination
13 restitution; making amends; paying money to those who have been wronged
16 smelling extremely unpleasant
17 to distinguish; to sift out; to separate out

Vocabulary Review
Lessons 121-130

Directions: Match each word with its best approximate definition. Note that definitions are not necessarily repeated verbatim from the lesson exercises.

1.	rudimentary	_____	a.	to disgust by excess sweetness or richness
2.	multifaceted	_____	b.	marked by or given to using irony in order to mock or convey contempt
3.	wax	_____	c.	involving or limited to basic principles
4.	cloying	_____	d.	to give an incentive or encouragement to; to push or propel along
5.	dumbfounded	_____	e.	a person or thing likely to cause harm or danger or threaten others
6.	vicarious	_____	f.	forbidden by laws, rules, or customs
7.	sarcastic	_____	g.	capable of working or living successfully
8.	viable	_____	h.	cheerful and carefree
9.	lighthearted	_____	i.	clever, original, or inventive
10.	pithy	_____	j.	experienced in the imagination through the feelings of another
11.	menace	_____	k.	reserved, modest, and shy
12.	illicit	_____	l.	to prevent or ward off
13.	venerate	_____	m.	a general feeling of discomfort, unease, or illness of which the exact cause is difficult to identify
14.	ingenious	_____	n.	greatly astonished or amazed at or by something
15.	demure	_____	o.	regard with great respect; revere
16.	spur	_____	p.	to make poor; to exhaust the strength or vitality of
17.	avert	_____	q.	having many qualities or faces
18.	impoverish	_____	r.	hard working; diligent
19.	sedulous	_____	s.	to become larger or stronger
20.	malaise	_____	t.	concise and forcefully expressive

Word Roots: Unit 13

ROOTS AND THEIR MEANINGS

man:	hand	dic:	to say, tell
clu/clo/cla:	to shut	anim:	life, spirit
ten:	hold, keep	esce:	to become

Here are a few examples of some words that use the above roots:

manual:
: done by hand; a handbook of instructions for learning to operate something

cloister:
: a convent or monastery (a place where one is shut up and shielded from the world for religious duties)

detention:
: the action of keeping someone in official custody; keeping one in school after hours

dictate:
: to lay down authoritatively; to say or read aloud

animation:
: a state of being lively and full of energy; creating a live movement out of successive drawings of things or out of puppets

coalesce:
: to come together and form a mass or a whole

Now try to fill in the table below by finding the appropriate root(s) and interpreting the meaning of each word:

Word	Root(s)	Guessed Meaning	Actual Meaning
predict			
retentive			
maneuver			
reclusive			
fluorescent			
animal			
claustrophobia			
amanuensis			
tenable			
conclude			

Lesson 131

FALLING APART

For many, the **stereotype** of a student who attends an elite university is that of a child who is **coddled** by his or her parents from the moment he or she is born. Often it is believed that such a student has delusions of **grandeur** and that this individual feels that he or she can do anything in the world. In reality, many students study very hard to attend top universities. They work **expeditiously** on many projects, are intensely involved with activities, and keep abreast of current affairs. Many such students can talk about anything from video games to economic theories to **truces** formed between nations that have ended major conflicts. And still these students work hard to survive. In reality, a good education is not only for the privileged; those who study hard can also achieve academic success.

NEW WORDS

coddle
ˈkädl

stereotype
ˈsterēəˌtīp, ˈsti(ə)r-

grandeur
ˈgranjər, ˈgranˌdyo͝or

expeditious
ˌekspəˈdiSHəs

truce
ˈtroōs

Definitions: Try matching the words in the list with the appropriate definitions. If you are stuck, check the glossary in the back of the book or the passage at the top of the page.

1. coddle   _____   a. being quick and still ensuring good result
2. stereotype   _____   b. an agreement between opponents to end their conflicts and discuss peace terms
3. grandeur   _____   c. to treat with excessive indulgence
4. expeditious   _____   d. (n.) commonly held idea or image about a specific group of people; (v.) treat with preconceived notion
5. truce   _____   e. quality of being impressive or splendid in style

Sentences: Try to use the words above in a sentence below. Remember that a word ending may be changed or its figure of speech slightly altered.

6. Asians are usually _____ as mathematically gifted in school.

7. The _____ of Angkor, an archaeological site that extends over 400 square kilometers, never fails to amaze tourists from all over the world.

8. The citizens living around the noisy construction site hope that it will be finished _____ so they can resume their peaceful lives.

9. Unlike European systems, Singapore's government does not _____ its citizens with welfare services and provides public assistance to the needy only sparingly.

10. Although a bilateral _____ between the two ethnic groups has been signed, it can be broken easily.

NEW WORDS

animate
ˈanəˌmit (adj.); ˈanəˌmāt (v.)

canvass
ˈkanvəs

gargantuan
gärˈganCHo͞oən

lax
laks

dilemma
diˈlemə

I looked around with caution, making sure that nobody was around while Madeline laboriously **canvassed** the **gargantuan** workroom of her fiancé. The security in the mansion was unusually **lax** tonight, so we had easily sneaked in. Madeline suspected that her fiancé had proposed to her solely out of guilt: he was a lawyer and he made a mistake in the past that led to her father's death. I knew how much Madeline loved her father; she always appeared **animated** whenever she talked about him. Madeline's **dilemma** was that she loved her fiancé, but was unsure whether she could forgive his past mistakes. But Madeline's doubt would remain unsubstantiated until she could find some legal evidence while rummaging through the room.

Definitions: Try matching the words in the list with the appropriate definitions. If you are stuck, check the glossary in the back of the book or the passage at the top of the page.

1.	animate	_____	a.	a difficult situation requiring a choice between two or more equally unfavorable options
2.	canvas	_____	b.	slipshod, not sufficiently strict or careful
3.	gargantuan	_____	c.	(adj.) alive or having life; (v.) 1. to bring to life or enliven; 2. to give renewed inspiration or encouragement to something
4.	lax	_____	d.	of great quantity; huge, giant
5.	dilemma	_____	e.	1. to try to obtain or request something, especially votes from people; 2. to try to get someone's opinion; 3. to discuss thoroughly

Sentences: Try to use the words above in a sentence below. Remember that a word ending may be changed or its figure of speech slightly altered.

6.   At night, Uncle Alan usually goes out to _____ construction sites for empty used bottles he collects and sells.

7.   Uyen is faced with a(n) _____: she has to choose between going to her best friend's wedding anniversary or her boyfriend's birthday party.

8.   Studying for final exams has triggered Tuan's _____ appetite for sweets, which help him release his stress.

9.   Looking at Lily's _____ eyes when admiring sculptures, one can sense her love for the art form.

10.   The condominium is thought to have _____ security because there have been only a few thieves who have managed to get away.

15

Lesson 133

RANDOMNESS

Christina chose an interesting hostel for our vacation in Penang: its interior design was primitive and ancient. Furthermore, some infrastructure was awfully **outdated**. When I asked Christina why she had chosen this hostel, she was **overt** about her intentions. She said that she wanted to **abstain** from a luxurious, modern lifestyle for a while. Then she went on to tell me that she had married a local man who would travel with her to Egypt and the Middle East. I was surprised by this **tangent**, but convinced that any story about marrying a random man had to be **fallacious**. But when Nasser walked into the room, I knew she was not lying.

Definitions: Try matching the words in the list with the appropriate definitions. If you are stuck, check the glossary in the back of the book or the passage at the top of the page.

1.	outdated	_____	a.	to resist doing something or to resist being tempted by something
2.	abstain	_____	b.	obsolete; no longer in trend
3.	tangent	_____	c.	done or shown openly; readily apparent
4.	overt	_____	d.	something based on a mistaken belief
5.	fallacious	_____	e.	a digression from the main topic

Sentences: Try to use the words above in a sentence below. Remember that a word ending may be changed or its figure of speech slightly altered.

6. Although many people write on their personal computers, a notebook and a pen will never become _____.

7. There are certain kinds of food you need to _____ from in your diet if you want to obtain a lean physique.

8. Dominique is very _____ about her feelings toward Nathan, although she tells her friends that she has no interest in him.

9. Bored of talking about the scientific names of organic molecules, Tai decided to go off on a(n) _____ and discuss the history of chemistry.

10. Because Malkah believed the _____ claim that it was Roman's birthday, she showed up with a birthday cake for him, to his bafflement.

Lesson 134

A QUIET CHARACTER

NEW WORDS

stoic
ˈstō-ik

acquiesce
ˌakwēˈes

posthumous
ˈpäsCHəməs, pästˈ(h)yo͞oməs

synopsis
səˈnäpsis

misanthrope
ˈmisənˌTHrōp, ˈmiz

Those who have only known Juan for a short time think of him as either a very **stoic** character or a **misanthrope**. He is not very vocal about his thoughts, but he expresses himself profusely in his writings. I had a chance to read a **synopsis** of one of his books and it has taught me more about Juan than a two-hour conversation with him. I know from his writing that Juan does not **acquiesce** to the social norms and he detests the idea of striving for **posthumous** fame as a writer.

Definitions: Try matching the words in the list with the appropriate definitions. If you are stuck, check the glossary in the back of the book or the passage at the top of the page.

1.	stoic	_____	a.	one who dislikes people in general
2.	acquiesce	_____	b.	calm, seemingly emotionless
3.	posthumous	_____	c.	to agree or give in
4.	synopsis	_____	d.	a brief summary or outline of a text
5.	misanthrope	_____	e.	happening after a person's death

Sentences: Try to use the words above in a sentence below. Remember that a word ending may be changed or its figure of speech slightly altered.

6.   The novel *The Love of The Last Tycoon* written by American author F. Scott Fitzgerald (1896-1940) was published _____ in 1941.

7.   Few people know how tough and _____ Tammy is because they are fooled by her petite figure and geniality.

8.   Despite Ray's wealth, he decided not to _____ to his wife's rising demand – she wanted a million dollar house.

9.   Trung is a full-scale _____: he never talks to people.

10.   "Here is the _____ of my play. I hope to hear your feedback."

17

Lesson 135

WHEN THINGS TURN SULLEN

Kyle was standing on the **precipice** contemplating jumping off. Those of us who watched knew that Kyle was depressed, and we **unanimously** begged him not to take the plunge. We told him that, with our support, he would **persevere** over any difficulties he may face in life. But Kyle did not listen and sent himself over the ledge. We all wept in silence, **conjoining** our sadness with a hope that the afterlife would provide Kyle more comfort. Then, suddenly, a miracle happened: Kyle floated through the air back up toward us. A **talisman** had given him the power of flight! We couldn't believe our eyes and rejoiced at the lucky trinket that Kyle beheld.

NEW WORDS

unanimous
yoo̅ˈnanəməs

precipice
ˈpresəpəs

persevere
ˌpərsəˈvi(ə)r

talisman
ˈtalismən, -iz-

conjoin
kənˈjoin, kän-

Definitions: Try matching the words in the list with the appropriate definitions. If you are stuck, check the glossary in the back of the book or the passage at the top of the page.

1. unanimous _____ a. to persist, to refuse to stop despite obstacles

2. precipice _____ b. two or more people in complete agreement, held by everyone involved

3. persevere _____ c. a very tall and steep cliff (literal or figurative)

4. talisman _____ d. to connect, to join

5. conjoin _____ e. an object (usually a stone, ring, or necklace) thought to possess magical powers

Sentences: Try to use the words above in a sentence below. Remember that a word ending may be changed or its figure of speech slightly altered.

6. Despite having been rejected by over thirty companies, Tung _____ and eventually landed his dream internship.

7. When standing at the _____ of the Grand Canyon, one can take beautiful pictures of the rock valleys, rivers, and ravines.

8. After deliberation, the jurors decided on a(n) _____ verdict to sentence the defendant.

9. According to a recent statistic, _____ twins occur about once in every 200,000 births.

10. Leandra found a(n) _____ that had the amazing ability to turn anything it directed its energy toward into gold.

NEW WORDS

discerning
diˈsərniNG

convergence
kənˈvərjəns

ambition
amˈbiSHən

affluence
ˈaflōōəns

transgression
transˈgreSHən, tranz-

Tai is an extremely bright businessman who has a knack for **discerning** lucrative opportunities that people usually overlook. His enormous **affluence** is undoubtedly due to a **convergence** of his great talents and his **ambition** to make lots of money. Yet Tai is by no means a greedy man. In fact, he holds venerable ethics and values and has never fallen into any **transgressions** during his pursuit of great wealth. He deems money only as a means to gain personal autonomy and to pursue worthy philanthropic endeavors.

Definitions: Try matching the words in the list with the appropriate definitions. If you are stuck, check the glossary in the back of the book or the passage at the top of the page.

1.	discerning	_____	a.	great wealth
2.	convergence	_____	b.	an act that violates a rule, law, or principle; an offense
3.	ambition	_____	c.	the act of coming together
4.	affluence	_____	d.	a strong desire to succeed
5.	transgression	_____	e.	perceptive, having good judgment; able to detect great subtlety

Sentences: Try to use the words above in a sentence below. Remember that a word ending may be changed or its figure of speech slightly altered.

6.   Beneath the global image of a(n) _____ Singapore, many citizens, especially those of the older generation, still suffer from great poverty.

7.   Hung and Alex do not get along well because there is no _____ of interests.

8.   Delilah's _____ sometimes exhausts her because she is always working hard to achieve her goals.

9.   Having practiced art for several years, Uyen has developed a(n) _____ eye for color.

10.   Having an affair is an unforgiveable _____ in a relationship.

Lesson 137

THE ODD ONE OUT

Having made many **concessions** to the demands of social norms, Jackson felt **jaded** and alienated from his true nature. He thought what is considered a social standard was **stymieing** his self-expression. Whenever he tried to be creative in **formulating** his unique lifestyle, he was met with **detractors** who called him an eccentric outcast.

Definitions: Try matching the words in the list with the appropriate definitions. If you are stuck, check the glossary in the back of the book or the passage at the top of the page.

1.	formulate	_____	a.	tired, lacking enthusiasm, or bored, usually after having too much of something
2.	stymie	_____	b.	to create methodically; articulate, express
3.	detractor	_____	c.	something granted in response to demands; a preferential allowance given by an organization or government
4.	concession	_____	d.	to hinder the progress of
5.	jaded	_____	e.	a person who criticizes or belittles the value of something

Sentences: Try to use the words above in a sentence below. Remember that a word ending may be changed or its figure of speech slightly altered.

6.   Writing essays all day long can leave even the most enthusiastic writer _____, depleted and uninspired.

7.   Vietnam's economic potential may be greatly _____ if the number of talented youth seeking opportunities overseas keeps increasing.

8.   Whenever I propose a new marketing idea, Joshua always finds fault in it and diminishes its effectiveness. What a(n) _____!

9.   Singapore's senior citizens and students can use public transportation at cheaper fares thanks to various transport _____ programs.

10.   It is difficult to _____ an opinion on the topic without knowing all of the facts.

NEW WORDS

compilation
ˌkämpəˈlāSHən

torpid
ˈtôrpid

summon
ˈsəmən

impressionistic
imˌpreSHəˈnistik

swarthy
ˈswôrTHē

Lesson 138

A PRACTICAL APPROACH

Ying has no **impressionistic** ideal of love and does not jump hastily into romance. After knowing that she is attracted to someone, Ying makes a thorough **compilation** of that person's history and personal strengths to see how he might fit into her life. Then she arranges to meet him regularly to ensure that he's not **torpid**, but rather lively during their conversations and activities together. After knowing for sure he is the right one (preferably a **swarthy** man), she **summons** up the courage to confess to him. Ying's approach may seem time-consuming at first but it helps her limit unproductive relationships in the long run.

Definitions: Try matching the words in the list with the appropriate definitions. If you are stuck, check the glossary in the back of the book or the passage at the top of the page.

1. compilation _____ a. based on unsystematic, subjective reactions
2. torpid _____ b. dark-skinned
3. summon _____ c. mentally or physically inactive; sluggish
4. impressionistic _____ d. a process or act of assembling different sources to put together something
5. swarthy _____ e. 1. to authoritatively or urgently call on someone or something to be present; 2. to call people to attend a meeting; 3. to urgently demand help; 4. to bring to the surface a quality or reaction from within oneself

Sentences: Try to use the words above in a sentence below. Remember that a word ending may be changed or its figure of speech slightly altered.

6. Alena made a potion and recited a mantra to _____ the spirits of her ancestors.

7. The record is a(n) _____ of my favorite soundtracks.

8. It is often easier to give _____ views than rational judgments.

9. When you compare citizens of Sweden to those of Sri Lanka, the Nordic people look much paler than their more _____ comrades in the tropics.

10. Kim has to _____ her courage in order to approach random strangers on the street to do her educational surveys.

Lesson 139

CONSOLATION

My heart and my head are inconsistent and sometimes are even in **disputation**. I wish to search for peace, but I act in a way that creates conflict. Sometimes, the consequences of my actions are so crushing that I become too emotionally affected. My mother would then remind me that it is only **mandatory** for the thunderstorm to come when there is an imbalance of electric charges and that after a gloomy night I can appreciate a **vividly** bright day better. For that, whenever I **wince** in time of great **despair**, I tell myself that a new source of joy, or direction, is about to arise.

Definitions: Try matching the words in the list with the appropriate definitions. If you are stuck, check the glossary in the back of the book or the passage at the top of the page.

1.	wince	_____	a.	hopelessness, pessimism
2.	despair	_____	b.	(n.) a facial or bodily response to suggest pain, distress; (v.) to recoil, draw back due to pain or fear
3.	vivid	_____	c.	required by rule, compulsory
4.	mandatory	_____	d.	debate or argument
5.	disputation	_____	e.	suggesting a clear and lively image; evoking strong feeling; intense in color

Sentences: Try to use the words above in a sentence below. Remember that a word ending may be changed or its figure of speech slightly altered.

6.   A(n) _____ illustration alongside a newspaper article can make the long reading appear less intimidating.

7.   It is _____ for international students to have immunization shots before coming to the United States for their studies.

8.   Don't give up in times of _____: things are not as bad as they seem at first.

9.   I _____ while trying to gulp down the blackish, pungent liquid that my parents called Chinese medicinal herbs but tasted to me like charcoal.

10.   It is surprising that Tung and An are dating because they used to be in constant _____.

NEW WORDS

muster
ˈməstər

haphazard
ˌhapˈhazərd

recessive
riˈsesiv

obdurate
ˈäbd(y)ərit

affable
ˈafəbəl

NATURE VERSUS NURTURE

While a trait such as attached earlobes is **recessive** in human beings, other qualities are not so definitively genetic. Take, for example, personality. Many people believe that, although genetics may play a role, it is much more likely that one's tendency to be **affable** or **obdurate** is governed by his or her upbringing and social experiences. As a result, psychologists and social workers have stressed the importance of making sure that children are reared in stable families where their emotional well-being is nurtured in a structured way. If a child is raised in a home with **haphazard** emotional organization, it will require that child additional effort to **muster** his or her strength to succeed in the world as an adult. Such goes the argument for those who believe that nurture, how one is raised, trumps nature, one's genetic inheritance, in society.

Definitions: Try matching the words in the list with the appropriate definitions. If you are stuck, check the glossary in the back of the book or the passage at the top of the page.

1.   muster   _____   a.   to assemble a group of people; to call up (a) feeling(s), emotion(s), or response(s)

2.   haphazard   _____   b.   genetic trait that is exhibited only when inherited from both parents

3.   recessive   _____   c.   unplanned, lacking organization

4.   obdurate   _____   d.   friendly, cordial

5.   affable   _____   e.   stubborn, resistant to change

Sentences: Try to use the words above in a sentence below. Remember that a word ending may be changed or its figure of speech slightly altered.

6.   Jin Hee is such a(n)_____ girl; everyone loves talking to her.

7.   The desired crystal structure cannot be obtained if the synthesis procedure is carried out _____ without order.

8.   She took a deep breath, _____ up her confidence, and entered the interview room.

9.   The two old men have been quarreling for months: a(n) _____ silence between them has persisted for weeks.

10.   Having blue eyes is a genetically _____ trait: unless both parents pass along an allele for blue eyes, a child will not have them.

Word Search

Lessons 131-140

```
N A E T A L U M R O F P R T
O C B C Q R U A C O O T L Q
I Q J M O S O A M S V D N S
T U P T T M N T T M I E U Y
A I U E Y V P H C S E O R Y
T E R N A D U I C A I L X T
U S O S A M A E L C R G I N
P C S B O N R M A A R T A D
S E D U D N I L B A T M E C
I E S I I U L M N I S I O D
D P C N P A R D O I T D O T
Q R G N F R E A L U D I L N
B M P N I U O A T L S R O G
B J K D R W T T E E W M K N
```

1 to treat with excessive indulgence
2 quality of being impressive or splendid in style
3 1. to try to obtain or request something, especially votes from people; 2. to try to get someone's opinion; 3. to discuss thoroughly
4 a difficult situation requiring a choice between two or more equally unfavorable options
5 done or shown openly; readily apparent
6 something based on a mistaken belief
7 to agree or give in
8 happening after a person's death
9 two or more people in complete agreement, held by everyone involved
10 an object (usually a stone, ring, or necklace) thought to possess magical powers
11 perceptive, having good judgment; able to detect great subtlety
12 a strong desire to succeed
13 to create methodically; articulate, express
14 a person who criticizes or belittles the value of something
15 a process or act of assembling different sources to put together something
16 mentally or physically inactive; sluggish
17 (n.) a facial or bodily response to suggest pain, distress; (v.) to recoil, draw back due to pain or fear
18 debate or argument
19 to assemble a group of people; to call up (a) feeling(s), emotion(s), or response(s)
20 stubborn, resistant to change

Vocabulary Review
Lessons 131-140

Directions: Match each word with its best approximate definition. Note that definitions are not necessarily repeated verbatim from the lesson exercises.

1. stereotype _____
2. truce _____
3. gargantuan _____
4. lax _____

5. outdated _____
6. abstain _____

7. synopsis _____

8. misanthrope _____
9. precipice _____

10. persevere _____

11. affluence _____

12. transgression _____

13. stymie _____

14. jaded _____
15. summon _____
16. swarthy _____
17. vivid _____

18. mandatory _____

19. haphazard _____

20. affable _____

a. a very tall, steep rock face or cliff
b. extremely large
c. wealth
d. to continue successfully in course of action, even with little hope of success
e. friendly, likeable
f. lacking any principle of organization; disorganized
g. to refrain oneself from doing or enjoying something
h. required
i. a brief summary of something
j. a widely held and oversimplified idea of a particular type of person or thing
k. to thwart; to hinder the progress of
l. to call on something; to demand; to call people to attend
m. an act that goes against the law or a code of conduct
n. dark-skinned
o. not strict with rules
p. bright, sharp, or clear
q. an agreement between enemies to stop fighting for a certain time
r. a person who dislikes humankind or who avoids human society
s. tired, bored, or lacking enthusiasm after having had too much of something
t. obsolete; out of date

25

Word Roots: Unit 14

ROOTS AND THEIR MEANINGS

dis:	apart, away from, not	**pun/pen:**	to pay, punish, compensate
nom/nym:	name	**us/ut:**	to use
gno:	to know	**un/non:**	not

Here are a few examples of some words that use the above roots:

disengaged: emotionally unattached
homonym: two or more words having the same spelling but different meanings
agnostic: a person who claims neither faith nor nonbelief in God
punitive: inflicting or intended to be punishment; a charge or tax that is exorbitantly high
utensil: an implement for household usage
uninspired: lacking in imagination, commitment, or originality
noncommittal: not willing to stick to a definite course of action

Now try to fill in the table below by finding the appropriate root(s) and interpreting the meaning of each word:

Word	Root(s)	Guessed Meaning	Actual Meaning
nomenclature			
penalty			
diagnostic			
unintelligent			
disrespectful			
reusable			
ignorant			
nonessential			
pseudonym			

NEW WORDS

rigorous
ˈrigərəs

blare
ble(ə)r

deluge
ˈdel(y)oōj

melodramatic
ˌmelədrəˈmatik

panorama
ˌpanəˈramə, -ˈrämə

Lesson 141

MOOD BREAKER

After hours of **rigorous** climbing, Chelsea and I finally reached the top of the mountain. A feeling of triumph swept over me as I gasped at the magnificent **panorama** in front of my eyes. The air was still and I felt almost engulfed by the vastness of the universe. Suddenly, Chelsea uttered in her usual **melodramatic** tone, "I've had a **deluge** of sweat and my feet are having peripheral oedema!" I turned to quiet her. In the serenity of nature, human voices sound like **blaring** car horns.

Definitions: Try matching the words in the list with the appropriate definitions. If you are stuck, check the glossary in the back of the book or the passage at the top of the page.

1.   rigorous   _____   a.   a wide, continuous view; an overall picture or thorough survey of something
2.   blare   _____   b.   (n.) a large amount of something coming at the same time; (v.) to flood with something
3.   deluge   _____   c.   painstaking and exact; demanding, harsh
4.   melodramatic   _____   d.   to make a loud, harsh noise
5.   panorama   _____   e.   exaggerated and overemotional

Sentences: Try to use the words above in a sentence below. Remember that a word ending may be changed or its figure of speech slightly altered.

6.   An ambitious student, Jake is always _____ with heavy schoolwork and club meetings.

7.   Marcus has a habit of wearing earphones that _____ loud music all the time, so he often cannot hear his friends when they call him from afar.

8.   Annabelle is usually pleasant, but her tendency to be a(n) _____ drama queen can be unbearable sometimes.

9.   To evaluate the significance of an artwork, one should consider the _____ of the work's historical context.

10.   Margaret Thatcher went through an academically _____ program in Chemistry at Oxford University before starting her career in politics.

27

Lesson 142

SERENDIPITY

Anh and Yuen met by serendipity. In a foreign city full of polished locals, they both dressed **slovenly** and thus quickly recognized each other as lone travelers. They came together and immediately clicked. They were able to **conjure** up **scintillating** conversations that energized each other's mind and to use their individual wisdom to **placate** each other's anxiety. They decided to keep accompanying one another because they both had a **prophetic** sense that a journey together would be more exciting and fulfilling.

Definitions: Try matching the words in the list with the appropriate definitions. If you are stuck, check the glossary in the back of the book or the passage at the top of the page.

1.	conjure	_____	a.	to calm, soothe, appease
2.	scintillating	_____	b.	ill-groomed and untidy; careless, negligent
3.	placate	_____	c.	shining brightly; clever and brilliant
4.	slovenly	_____	d.	accurately predictive of the future
5.	prophetic	_____	e.	to gather, to bring something into existence

Sentences: Try to use the words above in a sentence below. Remember that a word ending may be changed or its figure of speech slightly altered.

6. Estelle knew that her sister Harriet was difficult to _____, but it seemed that a trip to the baseball stadium had some effect on appeasing the latter.

7. Unlike Paula's _____ scholarship, which dazzles readers with ideas, Maureen's work is flat and boring.

8. Julia's living quarters were _____: dirty clothes were strewn about, stale food was left on the floor, and the bed sheets smelled foul.

9. People say that Jodi's words are _____ because her predictions have come true; but I'd rather think her warnings are based on rigorous reasoning.

10. It takes time for me to _____ up my courage to express my feelings for someone.

NEW WORDS

preponderance
pri'pändərəns

abject
'ab,jekt, ab'jekt

culpable
'kəlpəbəl

dissipate
'disə,pāt

subversive
səb'vərsiv

Lesson 143

A SUPPORTING HAND

She was sobbing uncontrollably. Tears welled up in her eyes which filled with a **preponderance** of **abject** sorrow. It had been one hour and her wails showed no sign of **dissipating**. I had never seen her so weak and vulnerable. She was always cool and composed. Something must have happened, a **subversive** event that sapped her usual vim. I asked her who was **culpable** of causing such sadness, but she refused to talk. Feeling helpless, I squeezed the side of her shoulder to offer my emotional support and she closed her eyes as she relished the feeling of compassion.

Definitions: Try matching the words in the list with the appropriate definitions. If you are stuck, check the glossary in the back of the book or the passage at the top of the page.

1. preponderance   _____   a.   being greater in number, importance, or quantity
2. abject   _____   b.   to be guilty and blameworthy for
3. culpable   _____   c.   to disperse; to waste away
4. dissipate   _____   d.   (adj.) attempting to undermine an established system; (n.) a revolutionist, insurgent
5. subversive   _____   e.   extremely miserable and unfortunate; contemptible, self-abashing

Sentences: Try to use the words above in a sentence below. Remember that a word ending may be changed or its figure of speech slightly altered.

6. There was a(n) _____ of chili peppers in my Thai dish; it was so spicy that I could barely eat it.

7. The evidence corroborated that Evan was indeed _____ of the crime.

8. Friction can cause energy to _____ in the form of heat.

9. Unfortunately, the national government is wary of _____ groups trying to overthrow or dislodge its power.

10. People flock to big cities like Saigon to search for new economic opportunities that will hopefully lift them up from _____ poverty.

Lesson 144

A WAY OF LIFE

Keefe is obsessed with handsome residences. He used to have a gorgeous house but he sold it to buy a cottage, and then sold the cottage for a villa where he is now living lavishly in **manorial** style. Keefe's parents are **enraged** by his spending habits and often advise him to find a less **obtrusive** way to show off his wealth. But Keefe has an **obstinate** view that money should be circulated instead of being hoarded. The **denotation** of money, to him, is only a medium of exchange. He believes he is exchanging papers for a lifestyle that makes him happy.

Definitions: Try matching the words in the list with the appropriate definitions. If you are stuck, check the glossary in the back of the book or the passage at the top of the page.

1.	obstinate	_____	a.	stubbornly persistent, unwilling to yield
2.	obtrusive	_____	b.	of or pertaining to a large country house with lands or the principal home of a landed estate (often in medieval times)
3.	enrage	_____	c.	noticeable or prominent in an unwelcome manner
4.	manorial	_____	d.	to make angry
5.	denotation	_____	e.	indication of something using words or symbols; the primary meaning of a word

Sentences: Try to use the words above in a sentence below. Remember that a word ending may be changed or its figure of speech slightly altered.

6.   Khang was a(n) _____ child who insisted on having his ways.

7.   Misophonia is a neuropsychiatric disorder in which specific sounds can _____ or disgust people who have the condition.

8.   Distinct from emotional connotation of words, _____ is their logical meaning.

9.   The best brand designs display subtlety and the logo is often not _____ showed.

10.   The _____ system, which was practiced in medieval Western societies, included the relationship between a landlord and a group of dependent peasants.

NEW WORDS

connotation
ˌkänəˈtāSHən

knell
nel

espouse
iˈspouz

penitent
ˈpenitnt

refined
riˈfīnd

Lesson 145

A PURSUIT OF PERFECTION

Yvonne **espouses** perfection because it energizes her. As such, she walks and behaves in a way that exudes an aura of **refined** elegance. Yvonne covets beautiful little things and scrutinizes everything she does and every word she says. For these reasons, she has built her brand, and the name Yvonne has a **connotation** among people around her. But Yvonne is a lonely soul. Men come and go because they are chased away by her unrealistic standards of perfection. For some, dating her is like tolling the death **knell** for their social lives. Nevertheless, even though Yvonne occasionally feels **penitent** about her choices, she has decided that she cannot give up her way of life.

Definitions: Try matching the words in the list with the appropriate definitions. If you are stuck, check the glossary in the back of the book or the passage at the top of the page.

1.	connotation	_____	a.	an idea or feeling that is implied or evoked by a term
2.	knell	_____	b.	to adopt and promote a cause, theory, or belief
3.	espouse	_____	c.	the sound of a bell, usually in reference to the dead or a funeral
4.	penitent	_____	d.	cultivated in manner, appearance, taste; free from impurities
5.	refined	_____	e.	repentant, regretful

Sentences: Try to use the words above in a sentence below. Remember that a word ending may be changed or its figure of speech slightly altered.

6.   The word "cancer" certainly does not have a positive _____.

7.   In regard to his taste for intellectual food, Tai is undeniably a very _____ man.

8.   A man and a woman should have similar family values that both _____ to ensure a stable marriage.

9.   Dinesh felt _____ because he lied to his mother, claiming that he took her money to pay for a college course when he actually burned the cash at a casino.

10.   In the town of Salem, the _____ of the church bell signals that a citizen has just passed away.

Lesson 146

UNCERTAINTY

When I agreed to go on that trip with him, I had a **presentiment** that it would not be all gain and no pain. I had **disjointed** ideas of who he was and he wasn't very **outspoken** about his feelings and thoughts. "Does he kidnap? Is he a good person? What will I do if bad things happen?" I was **plagued** with uncertainties because a few weeks of knowing him were insufficient to evaluate his character. Still, I could not possibly foresee every **contingency** that might take place during our trip. The only way to find out how things would turn out was to go ahead.

Definitions: Try matching the words in the list with the appropriate definitions. If you are stuck, check the glossary in the back of the book or the passage at the top of the page.

1.	disjointed	_____	a.	(n.) a thing or person that causes trouble and unhappiness; (v.) to cause distress
2.	plague	_____	b.	expressing one's opinion freely and frankly
3.	presentiment	_____	c.	divided, lacking continuity or organization
4.	outspoken	_____	d.	a possible event that might happen in the future; a provision for an unforeseen circumstance
5.	contingency	_____	e.	a gut feeling about the future, likely one of a foreboding nature

Sentences: Try to use the words above in a sentence below. Remember that a word ending may be changed or its figure of speech slightly altered.

6. Tina is _____ about her opinions so some of her colleagues do not like her.

7. We should have a(n) _____ plan if plan A does not work out.

8. I have a(n) _____ that our relationship will not last long due to our differences in characters and beliefs.

9. Keeping too much to oneself for a prolonged period of time might _____ one's emotional wellbeing.

10. Michael may sound smart and knowledgeable when talking about ecology but his understanding of the field is rather_____.

NEW WORDS

remiss
ri'mis

dispassionate
dis'paSHənit

temperate
'temp(ə)rət

seduce
si'd(y)oōs

brouhaha
'broōhä‚hä, broō'hähä

We sat next to each other, an icy silence hovering between us. She tried to break the ice by **seducing** me with food, but I remained **temperate**. She tried to get me talking by gossiping over some celebrity **brouhaha**, but I remained **dispassionate**. She tried to probe my thoughts by asking me questions, but I only nodded in silence. She then gave up and berated me for being aloof and **remiss** in politeness. Maybe she couldn't fathom how exhausted I felt as she was always energetic, or how deeply hurt I was that my blank mind couldn't muster up a response.

Definitions: Try matching the words in the list with the appropriate definitions. If you are stuck, check the glossary in the back of the book or the passage at the top of the page.

1.	remiss	_____	a.	uninfluenced by strong emotions
2.	dispassionate	_____	b.	negligent, careless in one's duty
3.	temperate	_____	c.	excited public response to something
4.	seduce	_____	d.	to lure someone into inadvisable courses of action or belief
5.	brouhaha	_____	e.	moderate; restrained in one's behavior

Sentences: Try to use the words above in a sentence below. Remember that a word ending may be changed or its figure of speech slightly altered.

6.   Joanie is trying to_____ Jake with her new line of perfume.

7.   Phong's teacher gave a lecture that was extremely _____: throughout the entire talk, Phong could hardly become engaged in the talk.

8.   "I don't care what other people think about my decisions", Ngoc said in a cold and _____ voice.

9.   We know we are _____ by distracting ourselves with movies and popcorn, but the writing assignments are too monotonous and unbearably dull.

10.   There was a(n) _____ over Julian's speech; it was full of wit but too casual and flippant for someone running for the student council's presidency.

Lesson 148

AMERICAN WOMEN'S VOTING RIGHTS

During her **grandiloquent** 1848 speech in Seneca Falls, New York, Elizabeth Cady Stanton (1815-1902) promoted a Declaration of Sentiments that would set in motion America's women's **suffrage** movement. This Declaration of Sentiments served as a **catalyst** that manifested a national movement to give women voting rights. As decades rolled on, ardent feminists **marshaled** support from fellow women and even some men to get equal political representation. Women finally were guaranteed voting rights in the United States in 1920. No longer a **prophecy**, women could actually begin voting in American elections after that year.

Definitions: Try matching the words in the list with the appropriate definitions. If you are stuck, check the glossary in the back of the book or the passage at the top of the page.

1.	prophecy	_____	a.	stimulus to make change happen
2.	marshal	_____	b.	prediction of future event
3.	suffrage	_____	c.	pompous in style or manner; designed in a way to impress
4.	catalyst	_____	d.	the right to vote
5.	grandiloquent	_____	e.	(n.) 1. an officer of the highest rank in the armed forces in certain countries; 2. a municipal officer or head of a police department; 3. an official responsible for supervising public events; (v.) to arrange or assemble in order

Sentences: Try to use the words above in a sentence below. Remember that a word ending may be changed or its figure of speech slightly altered.

6. My aunt believes blindly in _____; she is willing to pay lots of money to see a fortune-teller for half an hour.

7. Although many people enjoy hearing the politician's _____ speeches, I am turned off by the excessive indulgence of his parlance.

8. Iron is a commonly used _____ in organic chemical reactions.

9. For the past three months, the defendant's legal team has been attempting to _____ evidence proving that the defendant is indeed innocent.

10. Susan B. Anthony, an American social reformer, played an essential role in the women's _____ movement.

Lesson 149

CHARLES DARWIN

NEW WORDS

anthropological
anTHrəpəˈläjikə

rousing
ˈrouziNG

complicity
kəmˈplisitē

archipelago
ˌärkəˈpeləˌgō

exacting
igˈzaktiNG

Charles Darwin (1809-82) studied medicine and then divinity at Cambridge but neither discipline had as **rousing** an appeal to him as geology. In 1831, Darwin set off to the Galapagos Islands aboard the *HMS Beagle*, taking five weeks to make **exacting** charts of the **archipelago**. The voyage to the islands helped Darwin develop his theories of evolution, which he disclosed in his most famous book, *The Origin of Species* (1859). The implication of his theories led to the idea of Social Darwinism, an application of natural selection to sociology and politics, unfortunately without Darwin's full **complicity**. Also, Darwin's discussions on human evolution in his later books helped provide a foundation for modern biological **anthropology**.

Definitions: Try matching the words in the list with the appropriate definitions. If you are stuck, check the glossary in the back of the book or the passage at the top of the page.

1.	anthropological	_____	a.	relating to the study of humankind
2.	rousing	_____	b.	demanding great attention to detail
3.	complicity	_____	c.	inciting enthusiasm, full of energy
4.	archipelago	_____	d.	involvement with others in a crime or something illegal
5.	exacting	_____	e.	a group of islands

Sentences: Try to use the words above in a sentence below. Remember that a word ending may be changed or its figure of speech slightly altered.

6. Indonesia is a(n) _____ consisting of over 17,000 different islands.

7. After a(n) _____ celebration with her friends at the club, Kate went home and immersed herself in the stillness of the night.

8. Next week, our class is embarking on a(n) _____ expedition in northern India to investigate the local religious beliefs and practices.

9. I turned to his direction and signaled a wink of _____ between us.

10. One must give _____ attention to alignment and spacing in order to create an effective poster design.

Lesson 150

UNHAPPY LIFE

We love our auntie, except for her frequent and **irksome** lamenting. Auntie had enjoyed a privileged life, well protected by her loving parents, until she met my Uncle, who was raised in less **propitious** environment. Very often, she feels sore because her life is not **progressive**, and envious of her siblings because their wealth has greatly **surpassed** hers. Auntie's dissatisfaction with her current situation seems to make her more **peevish** nowadays.

Definitions: Try matching the words in the list with the appropriate definitions. If you are stuck, check the glossary in the back of the book or the passage at the top of the page.

1.	progressive	_____	a.	advancing gradually
2.	peevish	_____	b.	annoying in a tiresome way
3.	surpass	_____	c.	bad-tempered, tending to complain
4.	propitious	_____	d.	to go beyond expectations
5.	irksome	_____	e.	favorable; likely to result in success

Sentences: Try to use the words above in a sentence below. Remember that a word ending may be changed or its figure of speech slightly altered.

6. As you study vocabulary diligently every day, you should see a(n) _____ trend in your ability to read academic and intellectual work.

7. Francis's intuition and intellectual capacity for Physics far _____ that of his peers.

8. I find it really _____ when my brother keeps repeating one thing over and over again.

9. Song Woo is the most _____ woman I have ever met: almost everything can get under her skin.

10. Solid substrates in aquatic environment are _____ for the growth of fungus.

Crossword Puzzle
Lessons 141-150

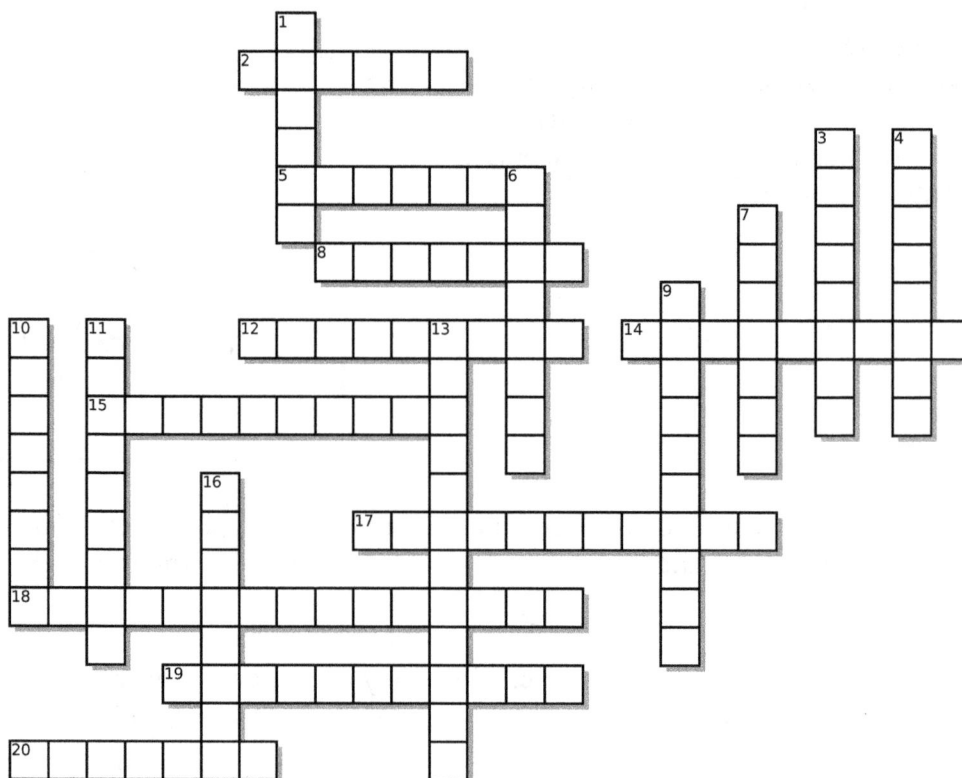

ACROSS

2 negligent, careless in one's duty
5 to gather, to bring something into existence
8 (n.) 1. an officer of the highest rank in the armed forces in certain countries; 2. a municipal officer or head of a police
12 to disperse; to waste away
14 accurately predictive of the future
15 (adj.) attempting to undermine an established system; (n.) a revolutionist, insurgent
17 an idea or feeling that is implied or evoked by a term
18 relating to the study of humankind
19 a possible event that might happen in the future; a provision for an unforeseen circumstance
20 to adopt and promote a cause, theory, or belief

DOWN

1 to lure someone into inadvisable courses of action or belief
3 prediction of future event
4 of or pertaining to a large country house with lands or the principal home of a landed estate (often in medieval times)
6 demanding great attention to detail
7 to go beyond expectations
9 favorable; likely to result in success
10 a wide, continuous view; an overall picture or thorough survey of something
11 stubbornly persistent, unwilling to yield
13 a gut feeling about the future, likely one of a foreboding nature
16 painstaking and exact; demanding, harsh

Vocabulary Review
Lessons 141-150

Directions: Match each word with its best approximate definition. Note that definitions are not necessarily repeated verbatim from the lesson exercises.

1.	blare	_____	a.	not influenced by strong emotion so as to be impartial and rational
2.	deluge	_____	b.	a flood of something
3.	scintillating	_____	c.	feeling sorrow or regret for having done something wrong
4.	slovenly	_____	d.	noticeable or prominent in an intrusive way
5.	preponderance	_____	e.	irritating; annoying
6.	culpable	_____	f.	to cause continual distress to; to pester and harass repeatedly
7.	obtrusive	_____	g.	elegant and cultured in appearance, manner, or taste
8.	enrage	_____	h.	a noisy, overexcited reaction in response to something
9.	penitent	_____	i.	a group of islands
10.	refined	_____	j.	a loud noise
11.	plague	_____	k.	favoring social/cultural reform of new, liberal ideas
12.	outspoken	_____	l.	the quality of being greater in quality, importance, or amount of something
13.	dispassionate	_____	m.	a person or thing that precipitates an event
14.	brouhaha	_____	n.	frank in stating one's opinions, especially if they're controversial
15.	suffrage	_____	o.	blameworthy, deserving of blame
16.	catalyst	_____	p.	the right to vote
17.	rousing	_____	q.	messy and dirty (usually of a person and his/her appearance)
18.	archipelago	_____	r.	exciting; stirring
19.	progressive	_____	s.	to make very angry
20.	irksome	_____	t.	sparkling or shining brightly

Word Roots: Unit 15

ROOTS AND THEIR MEANINGS

spec:	to look, appear	de:	away from, opposite of
gyn:	woman	tact:	touch
sed/sid:	to sit, be still	corp:	body

Here are a few examples of some words that use the above roots:

spectacle: a visually striking performance or play
misogynistic: referring to a hatred of women
sedentary: tending to spend much time seated down; inactive or inert
depart: to leave, often in order to embark on a journey
tactile: of or related to the sense of touch; tangible
corpse: a dead human body

Now try to fill in the table below by finding the appropriate root(s) and interpreting the meaning of each word:

Word	Root(s)	Guessed Meaning	Actual Meaning
deposit			
androgynous			
sediment			
corpus			
speculate			
preside			
contact			
detract			
retrospect			

Lesson 151

A CONCERN

"Do you think the media is reflecting our society in all its facets and complexity? I personally doubt that media **pluralism** is really free from influence."

"Why are you concerned?" Yadas responded.

"It is our right as citizens of a democratic society to be informed with news and perspectives, unaffected by political agenda and government **intrusion**." I **bemoaned**.

Yadas just shrugged his shoulders, saying nothing. I felt that it is only **pernicious** for societal development when we, the citizens, are disinterested and **lackadaisical**.

NEW WORDS

pluralism
ˈplo͝orəˌlizəm

bemoan
biˈmōn

intrusion
inˈtro͞oZHən

pernicious
pərˈniSHəs

lackadaisical
ˌlakəˈdāzikəl

Definitions: Try matching the words in the list with the appropriate definitions. If you are stuck, check the glossary in the back of the book or the passage at the top of the page.

1.	pluralism	_____	a.	to lament; to grieve
2.	bemoan	_____	b.	co-existence of groups of different backgrounds within one society
3.	intrusion	_____	c.	lacking enthusiasm or effort
4.	pernicious	_____	d.	unwelcome entrance which disturbs; something unwelcome
5.	lackadaisical	_____	e.	causing great harm, malicious

Sentences: Try to use the words above in a sentence below. Remember that a word ending may be changed or its figure of speech slightly altered.

6. There is no use _____ the amount of homework you are assigned; just get started and it will be all done in no time.

7. Taking advantage of people to make money may be lucrative at first but socially _____ in the long run.

8. How can Ziyi expect to get into a competitive medical school given her _____ attitude toward her studies?

9. I was aware of my _____ in Joanne's family but I had nowhere else to stay for the night and it was pouring outside.

10. In Montreal, there is cultural _____: people who speak French and people who speak English coexist and thrive in a beautiful metropolis.

NEW WORDS

stringent
ˈstrinjənt

decorous
ˈdekərəs, diˈkôrəs

pliable
ˈplīəbəl

vaccine
vakˈsēn

yen
yen

"Why are you always **decorous**? I find your **stringent** adherence to rules really boring," she said.

"You just want everyone to be **pliable** and playful and follow your wildness." I responded.

"Isn't it fun? Don't you have a **yen** to break free?"

"I am free within the constraints of my own principles."

"I find principles suffocating and pathogenic."

"Maybe you need a **vaccine**."

Definitions: Try matching the words in the list with the appropriate definitions. If you are stuck, check the glossary in the back of the book or the passage at the top of the page.

1.	stringent	_____	a.	keeping with good propriety and taste; polite and restrained
2.	decorous	_____	b.	rigorous, strictly controlled
3.	pliable	_____	c.	(n.) a strong yearning for something; (v.) to yearn for something
4.	vaccine	_____	d.	flexible, easily bent or molded
5.	yen	_____	e.	substance used to provide immunity against certain diseases; protective software

Sentences: Try to use the words above in a sentence below. Remember that a word ending may be changed or its figure of speech slightly altered.

6.   Dr. Lai is a(n) _____ lab technician: she practices safety vigorously and follows experimental procedures strictly.

7.   Vy always portrays a(n) _____ image of herself: she wears pretty dresses and acts extremely polite – even when she only goes shopping in the supermarket.

8.   I am open-minded, but my value system is in no way _____.

9.   It is advisable to have a full meal before taking doses of _____ so that your body has energy to fight the viruses.

10.   Tien has always had a(n) _____ to work as an art director.

Lesson 153

A LOVE FOR ORGANIC CHEMISTRY

Dr. Li, now the mother of two, often told her children about her time as a chemist at a **prestigious** research institution. She optimized mechanisms to synthesize **organic** compounds found in nature so they can be used in the medicinal industry. She recalled having to **maneuver** through a maze of possible intermediate pathways in order to produce the desired product. The synthesis procedure was rigorous; any **slipshod** handling of chemicals and miscalculations would result in considerable waste of time and resources. Although her job was demanding, Dr. Li found her discoveries and contributions to research **immensely** rewarding.

NEW WORDS

organic
ôr'ganik

immense
i'mens

slipshod
'slip‚SHäd

maneuver
mə'no͞ovər

prestigious
pre'stijəs, -'stē-

Definitions: Try matching the words in the list with the appropriate definitions. If you are stuck, check the glossary in the back of the book or the passage at the top of the page.

1.	organic	_____	a.	done in a careless manner
2.	immense	_____	b.	(n.) 1. a movement or series of movements requiring care and skill; 2. a carefully planned scheme often using deception; (v.) 1. to manipulate; 2. to turn or move skillfully
3.	slipshod	_____	c.	1. relating to living things; 2. produced without the use of chemical agents; 3. constitutional, essential as parts of a whole
4.	maneuver	_____	d.	having great reputation
5.	prestigious	_____	e.	extremely strong, in great quantity

Sentences: Try to use the words above in a sentence below. Remember that a word ending may be changed or its figure of speech slightly altered.

6. Instead of enjoying learning at his own pace, Zhang viewed high school as a rat race to earn an acceptance letter from a(n) _____ university.

7. I have never seen any scholarship application essay that was written in such a(n) _____ manner!

8. Anh cried, unable to hide her _____ and happy emotions when she reunited with her son after four years.

9. Food that is labeled _____ is sold at a higher price, but its actual nutritional contents may just be as good as the non-organic food.

10. Koh has a knack for _____ people to do what she wants; be careful when you are with her.

NEW WORDS

laborious
lə'bôrēəs

averse
ə'vərs

adhere
ad'hi(ə)r

spate
spāt

hedonistic
ˌhēdn'istik

AN EPICUREAN

Joel is an undisciplined and **hedonistic** spirit. He takes great delight in sensuous enjoyment of food and drinks and treats every day as a vacation. He is **averse** to **laborious** tasks that require great effort from him. Although Joel has many creative ideas for his independent projects, whenever a **spate** of work arises, he would procrastinate by distracting himself with movies and would be unable to **adhere** to any disciplined schedule to get his projects accomplished. With such attitude, Joel is currently unemployed. I wonder how he can fund his pursuit of pleasures.

Definitions: Try matching the words in the list with the appropriate definitions. If you are stuck, check the glossary in the back of the book or the passage at the top of the page.

1.	laborious	_____	a.	to stick to firmly; to follow through	
2.	averse	_____	b.	seeking pleasure, especially for self-indulgence	
3.	adhere	_____	c.	arduous, demanding great effort and time	
4.	spate	_____	d.	strongly opposed to	
5.	hedonistic	_____	e.	a large number or amount of something happening in quick succession	

Sentences: Try to use the words above in a sentence below. Remember that a word ending may be changed or its figure of speech slightly altered.

6.   Singapore Architecture students often spend _____ hours in the design studios and thus are seldom present at social events.

7.   A(n) _____ wife is difficult to please: she always wants more clothes, shoes and expensive vacations.

8.   It is important to _____ strictly to the laboratory safety rules to minimize the risks of accidents.

9.   A(n) _____ of consecutive failed attempts really challenges one's patience and tenacity.

10.   Don't be _____ to constantly challenging your comfort zone because that attitude will help you grow.

Lesson 155

A TASTELESS MEAL

We had a habit of discussing work over meals because eating good food was our outlet to regain clarity of thought. Somehow this time, the **succulent** dishes provided little help to our **unhinged** minds.

"The legal case we are handling is particularly **tedious**. Right now, we only have **presumptive** evidence, but it's neither conclusive nor sufficient to file our lawsuit. We need more time to investigate. It's easy to lapse into a **provincial** perspective under time pressure."

He said while I nodded in agreement, thinking how tasteless the food was.

NEW WORDS

succulent
ˈsəkyələnt

provincial
prəˈvinSHəl

presumptive
priˈzəmptiv

unhinge
ˌənˈhinj

tedious
ˈtēdēəs

Definitions: Try matching the words in the list with the appropriate definitions. If you are stuck, check the glossary in the back of the book or the passage at the top of the page.

1.	succulent	_____	a.	taking something to be true or adopting a particular attitude toward something
2.	provincial	_____	b.	juicy and tasty
3.	presumptive	_____	c.	1. to make someone mentally unbalanced; 2. to deprive of stability or fixity; 3. to take a door off its hinges
4.	unhinge	_____	d.	boring and tiresome due to dull repetition
5.	tedious	_____	e.	narrow-minded, unsophisticated

Sentences: Try to use the words above in a sentence below. Remember that a word ending may be changed or its figure of speech slightly altered.

6. Making a good moussaka can be a really _____ task: there are more than 10 intermediate steps in the recipe before the final dish is prepared.

7. I'm having a craving for a(n) _____ salmon fillet carpeted in cream mushroom sauce accompanied by a glass of champagne for dinner.

8. After Claire had received a phone call from her cousin, her mind became _____ and she couldn't focus on her work any more.

9. He found the people in the city ostentatious, and they found him _____, uneducated, and detached.

10. Tal was _____ in assuming that her housemate had stolen her money without having searched her room for the lost cash.

NEW WORDS

audacious
ô'dāSHəs

exempt
ig'zem(p)t

alienate
'ālēə,nāt, 'ālyə-

faction
'fakSHən

disparity
di'sparitē

In a few hours, I will know which **faction** I belong to: the gifted or the mediocre. Our school divides the kids into these two classes of great **disparity** by an aptitude test so that the teachers can best cater to our different needs. I am not in a position to challenge this established system, but I feel that the students in one group are **alienated** from those in the other. The teachers also tend to be more lenient and make more **exemptions** for the gifted ones. There are probably students who have similar views but none of us is **audacious** enough to voice our opinions.

Definitions: Try matching the words in the list with the appropriate definitions. If you are stuck, check the glossary in the back of the book or the passage at the top of the page.

1.   audacious   _____   a.   to make someone feel isolated or estranged
2.   exempt   _____   b.   bold, daring
3.   alienate   _____   c.   a small dissenting group within a larger group, especially in politics
4.   faction   _____   d.   a great difference between things
5.   disparity   _____   e.   (adj.) free from liability or obligation imposed on others; (n.) a person who is free of liability for something, usually paying tax; (v.) to free a person from an obligation or liability imposed on others

Sentences: Try to use the words above in a sentence below. Remember that a word ending may be changed or its figure of speech slightly altered.

6.   Artists are thought to have _____ souls because they seem to be in their world and away from the public while creating their best work.

7.   When you compare Yolanda's elegant mansion to Mark's dilapidated bungalow, the _____ between the quality of the two homes is unmistakable.

8.   As a foreign student studying in Singapore, I was _____ from taking a course in a second language.

9.   Jacob had a lot of _____ to throw confetti and play celebration music at his uncle's funeral.

10.   Stereotyping and a lack of understanding can lead to _____ within a group.

Lesson 157

A CHILDHOOD GAME

As children, my brother and I liked to role-play. One time, we assumed ourselves to be imaginative political characters **segregated** by different ideologies. One of us was kind and pro-environment while the other, acting with great **turpitude**, had no issue destroying nature's wonders. We debated hotly over how to manage our **parched** national forests. But we were only children. Because we were young, our discussion hardly **elucidated** any important environmental questions and our proposed solutions were too simple to solve any complex problems. Sometimes we fell into disputations so intense that our mother had to step in for **mediation**. My brother is now in law school, perhaps due to the influence of our childhood experience.

NEW WORDS

segregation
ˌsegriˈgāSHən

mediation
ˌmēdēˈāSHən

parch
pärCH

elucidate
iˈloōsiˌdāt

turpitude
ˈtərpiˌt(y)oōd

Definitions: Try matching the words in the list with the appropriate definitions. If you are stuck, check the glossary in the back of the book or the passage at the top of the page.

1.	segregation	_____	a.	to clarify; to illuminate
2.	mediation	_____	b.	act of intervention to resolve conflicts
3.	parch	_____	c.	depravity; wickedness
4.	elucidate	_____	d.	to dry something completely through heat
5.	turpitude	_____	e.	separation into groups

Sentences: Try to use the words above in a sentence below. Remember that a word ending may be changed or its figure of speech slightly altered.

6.   Rosanne's language is esoteric and philosophical and I often need to ask her to _____ what she means.

7.   Some believe that peace in the Middle East is still possible, but only through unbiased _____.

8.   An effective leader will encourage inclusiveness and avoid _____ among his people.

9.   Saigon's weather in April is so hot that I feel as if my skin will be as _____ as dried weed if I go out under the sun.

10.   The dictator's _____ shocked everyone: any citizen that disagreed with his views was swiftly executed.

NEW WORDS

acoustic
əˈko͞ostik

doctrinaire
ˌdäktrəˈner

impecunious
ˌimpəˈkyo͞onēəs

plunge
plənj

escalate
ˈeskəˌlāt

Lesson 158

FROM ACADEMIA TO BUSINESS

Marge spent eight years in graduate school studying **acoustic** patterns in medieval Celtic music. But when she finished her degree, she was unable to find an academic job. Under such circumstances, she was forced to take a **plunge** into a pragmatic career. Initially, employers had no interest in hiring Marge because her **doctrinaire** interview answers held little practicality. As a result, Marge grew anxious because she feared that she would never be hired and that she would live an **impecunious** lifestyle for decades. So she **escalated** her efforts to get a job by learning some practical technical skills. Now she is the CFO of a large technology company in California.

Definitions:　　Try matching the words in the list with the appropriate definitions. If you are stuck, check the glossary in the back of the book or the passage at the top of the page.

1.	acoustic	_____	a.	insistent on using theory or doctrine without considering practicality
2.	doctrinaire	_____	b.	relating to sound, hearing
3.	impecunious	_____	c.	to become more serious and intense
4.	plunge	_____	d.	having little or no money
5.	escalate	_____	e.	(n.) a jump or dive into water; 2. a swift and drastic fall in value or amount; (v.) 1. to move downward or drop steeply; 2. to embark on something with vigor

Sentences:　　Try to use the words above in a sentence below. Remember that a word ending may be changed or its figure of speech slightly altered.

6.　Some people prefer _____ renditions of pop songs to their original versions.

7.　A trivial disagreement between a bus driver and a passenger quickly _____ into a serious dispute.

8.　Morton led a(n) _____ lifestyle; he saved endlessly for items because he could barely afford to survive.

9.　When Tom saw snow for the first time, he got super excited and immediately _____ into that thick white blanket.

10.　Unlike Ethan, who was very pragmatic in his approach to solving traffic problems, Carlo maintained a(n) _____ mindset.

Lesson 159

ANOTHER WAY

I joked and she laughed. I could tell from her outbursts of **mirth** that she was in a **transitory** state of joy. But her deep grey eyes possessed a **perpetual** sadness. Eyes don't lie; they have an **intrinsic** ability to converse in a way words alone cannot convey. I wanted to connect with her beyond our laughter so I reached out for her hands and my eyes fixated at hers, as if inviting a more **holistic** conversation.

Definitions: Try matching the words in the list with the appropriate definitions. If you are stuck, check the glossary in the back of the book or the passage at the top of the page.

1.	holistic	_____	a.	considering all factors, all-inclusive
2.	intrinsic	_____	b.	fleeting, not lasting
3.	mirth	_____	c.	amusement – often expressed by laughter
4.	perpetual	_____	d.	inherent, innate, essential
5.	transitory	_____	e.	occurring repeatedly; lasting forever

Sentences: Try to use the words above in a sentence below. Remember that a word ending may be changed or its figure of speech slightly altered.

6.   Colleges claim that undergraduate admission is _____: not only grades and test scores are assessed, but essays, activities, references, and character also play a role in accepting an applicant.

7.   Apart from external motives, it is important that one find _____ joy and meaning in what one does.

8.   The city seems to be in _____ transformation: there is always something new every now and then.

9.   Happiness is only a(n) _____ feeling.

10.   Everyone loves to be with people who bring laughter and _____.

NEW WORDS

incidental
ˌinsiˈdentl

linchpin
ˈlinCHˌpin

commend
kəˈmend

surmount
sərˈmount

fouled
fould

Lesson 160

AUNT KARINA

Aunt Karina was the **linchpin** that held the family together. It seemed like, with her support, there was no obstacle that I or my siblings could not **surmount**. Even with only **incidental** information about our travesties, Karina could give us fabulous guidance. Each of us in the family **commended** her for her prescience and kindness to help us navigate rough waters. Her reputation among members of our family never **fouled**.

Definitions: Try matching the words in the list with the appropriate definitions. If you are stuck, check the glossary in the back of the book or the passage at the top of the page.

1. incidental _____ a. occurring as a consequence; secondary, subordinate
2. linchpin _____ b. made dirty, defiled, or soiled
3. commend _____ c. to overcome; to get over something
4. surmount _____ d. to praise; to endorse
5. fouled _____ e. a person or thing vital to a business or an organization

Sentences: Try to use the words above in a sentence below. Remember that a word ending may be changed or its figure of speech slightly altered.

6. Lindy is seen as the _____ that holds her billiards team together: if she quit, then the entire team would dissolve.

7. Intense physical attraction is only _____ to building a stable and meaningful relationship.

8. Don't make contemptible decisions that will make your reputation become _____.

9. Being clear of the upcoming challenges that have to be _____ in order to achieve your goals will get you ready mentally.

10. Amy should be _____ for the countless hours that she has devoted to helping the poor in New York City.

49

Word Search

Lessons 151-160

```
S Z B T R R N V Z T L Y J D F Q T
V U D R X B N G G K E N V A M Q W
S U O I N U C E P M I D C M Z D X
Y P T I M M K R D N V T I P W T R
D R E T G Q Y Q L U I B D O Y Z Z
E D O R X I L B C O T E G N U L P
C T Z T P G T A N I X I Z B L S T
O T I Y I E J S B N N M P L B P R
R P H N P S T N E O N A G R P B S
O M C P T E N U I R R M G L U U T
U E R Y T R E A A P P I U R R T E
S X A A D N U B R L H R O M O G J
Z E P J I T N S G T A C O U N B Q
Y S N C L Q W M I L N U N I S J Q
L Y C L R J Q J I O N J H I V L P
G A M W P N L S Y T N N R D L Y D
V P K Z J Z M J G B U T W M Z L Y
```

1 co-existence of groups of different backgrounds within one society
2 unwelcome entrance which disturbs; something unwelcome
3 keeping with good propriety and taste; polite and restrained
4 substance used to provide immunity against certain diseases; protective software
5 1. relating to living things; 2. produced without the use of chemical agents; 3. constitutional, essential as parts of a whole
6 having great reputation
7 arduous, demanding great effort and time
8 a large number or amount of something happening in quick succession
9 1. to make someone mentally unbalanced; 2. to deprive of stability or fixity; 3. to take a door off its hinges
10 boring and tiresome due to dull repetition
11 (adj.) free from liability or obligation imposed on others; (n.) a person who is free of liability for something, usually paying tax; (v.) to free a person from an obligation or liability imposed on others
12 a small dissenting group within a larger group, especially in politics
13 to dry something completely through heat
14 depravity; wickedness
15 having little or no money
16 (n.) a jump or dive into water; 2. a swift and drastic fall in value or amount; (v.) 1. to move downward or drop steeply; 2. to embark on something with vigor
17 occurring repeatedly; lasting forever
18 fleeting, not lasting
19 a person or thing vital to a business or an organization
20 to overcome; to get over something

Vocabulary Review
Lessons 151-160

Directions: Match each word with its best approximate definition. Note that definitions are not necessarily repeated verbatim from the lesson exercises.

1. pernicious _____
2. lackadaisical _____
3. stringent _____
4. pliable _____
5. immense _____
6. maneuver _____
7. averse _____
8. hedonistic _____
9. succulent _____
10. provincial _____
11. audacious _____
12. alienate _____
13. segregation _____
14. elucidate _____
15. doctrinaire _____
16. escalate _____
17. holistic _____
18. mirth _____
19. incidental _____
20. fouled _____

a. lazy; lacking enthusiasm and determination
b. easily bent or influenced; flexible
c. to cause to become more intense or serious
d. in the pursuit of self-pleasure, usually self-indulgent
e. accompanying but not a major part of something
f. having a strong dislike or opposition to something
g. the act of setting someone or something apart from others
h. cause someone to feel isolated or estranged
i. seeking to impose a belief in a circumstance without regard to practical considerations
j. characterized by the parts being referenced or explicable only in consideration of the whole
k. having a harmful effect, especially in a gradual or subtle way
l. amusement, often expressed by laughter
m. bold and daring, perhaps with a lack of respect
n. concerning a person or place: narrow minded or unsophisticated
o. to twist, turn, or manipulate
p. strict, precise, and exacting (of regulations and conditions)
q. to make something clear; explain
r. extremely large or great, especially in scale or degree
s. offensive smelling; wicked or immoral
t. juicy, tender, or tasty (of a food)

Word Roots: Unit 16

ROOTS AND THEIR MEANINGS

retro:	backward, behind	**simil/simul:**	likeness, imitation
cis:	to cut	**am:**	to love
urb:	city	**co/com/con:**	with, together

Here are a few examples of some words that use the above roots:

retrograde:	movement that is directed backward
scissors:	implement or instrument used to cut materials
urban:	concerning or relating to a city or a town
simultaneous:	occurring, happening, or operating at the same time
amorous:	showing, feeling, or relating to sexual desire
connect:	to join together so that a link (either literally or figuratively) is established

Now try to fill in the table below by finding the appropriate root(s) and interpreting the meaning of each word:

Word	Root(s)	Guessed Meaning	Actual Meaning
simulate			
combine			
retroactive			
cooperate			
retrospect			
amicable			
suburbia			
incision			

NEW WORDS

morass
mə'ras, mô-

auditory
'ôdiˌtôrē

refract
ri'frakt

adamant
'adəmənt

righteous
'rīCHəs

MITCHELL'S MADNESS

Mitchell went to his doctor and **adamantly** demanded that the latter terminate his prescription medication, as the side effects made him feel nauseous. The doctor reminded him that the last time Mitchell had stopped taking his medication, his psychotic symptoms had quickly returned, leaving him in a **morass** of delusional problems. For example, Mitchell would notice that light would **refract** to create face-like shadows on the wall, and he would also hear **auditory** hallucinations of angry voices from the wall shouting at him. After being reminded of this, Mitchell began to second-guess himself. He knew that his doctor was a trustworthy professional and a **righteous** man, who only wanted what was best for his patients, so Mitchell agreed to continue taking his medication despite the unwanted side-effects.

Definitions: Try matching the words in the list with the appropriate definitions. If you are stuck, check the glossary in the back of the book or the passage at the top of the page.

1. morass   _____ a. to make a ray of light change direction when it enters a medium at an angle goes through at an angle

2. auditory   _____ b. morally right or justifiable
3. refract   _____ c. 1. an area of boggy ground; 2. a complicated or confusing situation
4. adamant   _____ d. relating to the sense of hearing
5. righteous   _____ e. refusing to be persuaded

Sentences: Try to use the words above in a sentence below. Remember that a word ending may be changed or its figure of speech slightly altered.

6. Although his colleagues pointed out many flaws in his business plan, Adam remained _____ about going through with it.

7. The physics teacher amazed his students when he showed them how lenses _____ light differently depending on what they are made of.

8. Harold navigated through the _____ of having both of his ex-girlfriends tell him that he was a bad boyfriend at once every night for a week.

9. Helen was a visual learner; she could remember everything she read but could not seem to absorb _____ information at all.

10. A(n) _____ person can be trusted to make fair decisions even in difficult situations.

Lesson 162

YEAR OF THE GOAT

Residents of New York City's Chinatown recently hosted a parade for the Chinese New Year, an event that celebrates the rich cultural **heritage** of the Chinese people. However, in an act of deplorable **jingoism**, a group of intolerant citizens attempted to ruin the celebration by trying to **dislodge** the head of a goat (a **figurative** manifestation of the new year) that had been constructed for the parade. Much to the jingoists' **chagrin**, police stopped them before they succeeded, and the parade continued as planned.

NEW WORDS

dislodge
dis'läj

chagrin
SHə'grin

jingoism
'jiNGgō,izəm

heritage
'heritij

figurative
'figyərətiv

Definitions: Try matching the words in the list with the appropriate definitions. If you are stuck, check the glossary in the back of the book or the passage at the top of the page.

1.   dislodge   _____   a.   distress or embarrassment at having failed or been humiliated

2.   chagrin   _____   b.   1. property that is inherited; 2. objects or traditions, values, historical buildings or countryside passed down from previous generations

3.   jingoism   _____   c.   to knock or force out of position

4.   heritage   _____   d.   metaphorical, not literal

5.   figurative   _____   e.   extreme patriotism

Sentences: Try to use the words above in a sentence below. Remember that a word ending may be changed or its figure of speech slightly altered.

6.   The death of his father was heartbreaking, but the property he received as part of his _____ would keep him financially afloat while he grieved.

7.   Max managed to _____ one of his teeth after getting hit in the mouth with a basketball during recess.

8.   Owen's acne problem was a constant source of _____ throughout his high school years.

9.   My comment wasn't supposed to be taken literally! I was speaking in a(n) _____ manner in order to illustrate my point more powerfully.

10.   Having national pride may sometimes be admirable, but _____ can result in negative attitudes towards certain nationalities.

NEW WORDS

stimulate
ˈstimyəˌlāt

rigid
ˈrijid

predilection
ˌpredlˈekSHən, ˌprēdl-

tenet
ˈtenit

palliate
ˈpalēˌāt

Lesson 163

ARTHRITIC GARY

Gary had a strong desire to take up Buddhist meditation, as he believed that following the **tenets** and practices of Buddhism would give him more peace in his life and help him reduce his **predilections** towards unhealthy habits. However, his arthritis caused his knees to hurt whenever he tried to fold his **rigid** legs into a cross-legged seated position. His physician told him that regular stretching to **stimulate** his knees daily would help ease the pain when getting into this position. Indeed, the stretching exercises did **palliate** the situation, but the arthritis was still there, so Gary decided to try lying-down meditation instead.

Definitions: Try matching the words in the list with the appropriate definitions. If you are stuck, check the glossary in the back of the book or the passage at the top of the page.

1.	stimulate	_____	a.	a preference or special liking for something
2.	rigid	_____	b.	to make less severe or unpleasant without removing the cause
3.	predilection	_____	c.	a principle or belief
4.	tenet	_____	d.	to make (something) more active or excited
5.	palliate	_____	e.	unable to bend or be forced out of shape

Sentences: Try to use the words above in a sentence below. Remember that a word ending may be changed or its figure of speech slightly altered.

6.   The cat's body became as _____ as a board when it heard the neighbor's dog let out a vicious bark.

7.   Before she even asked him where he would like to eat, Lindsey knew Jim would suggest a Mexican restaurant due to his _____ for spicy tacos.

8.   Leyla joined a yoga class in hopes of _____ her chronic back pain, but she knew she would need surgery if she wanted to get rid of it permanently.

9.   According to the Bible, the Ten Commandments are eternal _____ that serve as a guide to basic morality.

10.   The children became very _____ and could not be calmed down after eating all of their holiday candy at once.

55

Lesson 164

LOUIE MISSES NEW YORK

As a child of lower Manhattan, Louie never enjoyed living in Texas. He grew **disenchanted** with Texas' rustic lifestyle and yearned to return to the big city. One day he grew **despondent** enough to listen to his friend Janet, a fellow New Yorker who had been **appraising** his unfortunate situation. "I'll tell you what," she said. **Blandishing** him with an offer, she continued, "It seems like life here is **noxious** for you. If you come to New York, I will give you half off rent in my apartment." Louie was enthralled and Janet was too, for she had a secret crush on Louie and still earned money off of a business transaction.

Definitions: Try matching the words in the list with the appropriate definitions. If you are stuck, check the glossary in the back of the book or the passage at the top of the page.

1.	disenchanted	_____	a.	to assess the value or quality of
2.	despondence	_____	b.	harmful; poisonous; extremely unpleasant
3.	appraise	_____	c.	to coax with kind words or flattery
4.	blandish	_____	d.	a state of low spirits due to loss of hope or courage
5.	noxious	_____	e.	disappointed by someone or something previously respected or admired

Sentences: Try to use the words above in a sentence below. Remember that a word ending may be changed or its figure of speech slightly altered.

6.   Tom tried to _____ his tutor into telling his parents he was a responsible student when he did not do his work.

7.   Fans became _____ with the band after the release of their new album, which was drastically different in sound compared to their previous work.

8.   Often people find the smell of a skunk to be _____; it is extremely odorous and unsettling.

9.   Paulina's _____ over the loss of her beloved pet dog showed no sign of letting up anytime soon.

10.   Michael was known for _____ potential employees rather stringently during their interviews.

NEW WORDS

luxury
'ləkSH(ə)rē, 'ləgZH(ə)-

vulgar
'vəlgər

decisive
di'sīsiv

aggrandize
ə'gran͵dīz

precede
pri'sēd

Lesson 165

TURNING THINGS AROUND

Liam grew up in a poor family that lived a **vulgar**, destitute life. Even simple things that many people take for granted, such as having heat during the winter, were **luxuries** for them. However, as Liam grew up, he took **decisive** action in order to **aggrandize** his and his family's situation. Unlike the generations in his family that **preceded** him, Liam decided to take his education seriously so that he could attend university and eventually start his own business to support himself and help his struggling parents.

Definitions: Try matching the words in the list with the appropriate definitions. If you are stuck, check the glossary in the back of the book or the passage at the top of the page.

1.	luxury	_____	a.	able to make choices quickly and/or confidently
2.	vulgar	_____	b.	to happen or come before (in time)
3.	decisive	_____	c.	1. a state of extravagant living; 2. an inessential desirable item that is expensive
4.	aggrandize	_____	d.	lacking sophistication or good taste
5.	precede	_____	e.	to make great or greater

Sentences: Try to use the words above in a sentence below. Remember that a word ending may be changed or its figure of speech slightly altered.

6. Although their children love listening to rap music, many parents find the _____ language prevalent in rap lyrics to be offensive.

7. When appointing a leader, it is important to choose a(n) _____ person that can act without worrying about every possible consequence.

8. The townspeople hoped that the newly elected mayor would be more effective than the person that _____ him.

9. Jay dreamed of the life of_____ he would lead if he were ever lucky enough to win the lottery.

10. The president hoped that his new healthcare policy would _____ his public image.

Lesson 166

ALIEN ATTACK

Steven's favorite movie is an indie sci-fi film called *Attack of the Blobs*. The movie is about the introduction of an **invasive** alien species on Earth that eventually brings about an **apocalypse**. When the aliens first land on the planet, they are tiny, seemingly harmless creatures that are incapable of causing even the smallest **mischief**. However, over the span of a few days, their bodies grow into gigantic, **amorphous** blobs that destroy the streets and buildings with which they came into contact. After **zealously** sending in military forces to successfully halt alien destruction, the government enacted a new policy that involved the immediate termination of any foreign species that arrived upon domestic soil.

NEW WORDS

apocalypse
əˈpäkəˌlips

mischief
ˈmisCHif

zealous
ˈzeləs

invasive
inˈvāsiv

amorphous
əˈmôrfəs

Definitions: Try matching the words in the list with the appropriate definitions. If you are stuck, check the glossary in the back of the book or the passage at the top of the page.

1.	apocalypse	_____	a.	extremely passionate about or devoted to (sometimes in a negative way)
2.	mischief	_____	b.	1. a great disaster; 2. the end of the world
3.	zealous	_____	c.	without clearly defined shape or form
4.	invasive	_____	d.	playful misbehavior or troublemaking
5.	amorphous	_____	e.	tending to spread undesirably or harmfully

Sentences: Try to use the words above in a sentence below. Remember that a word ending may be changed or its figure of speech slightly altered.

6. Children will often get into_____ if there is no one watching them.

7. Pete's new band had a(n) _____ lineup; it was constantly changing and had no permanent members.

8. Scientists are trying their best to warn the world of the inclement environmental _____ that will occur if global warming is not taken seriously.

9. As one of the most _____ Fleetwood Mac fans I know, Stevie has band posters, tickets, and albums posted all over her room.

10. The sound of the construction was quite _____ and could be heard in every building on the block.

NEW WORDS

libertine
ˈlibərˌtēn

cerebral
səˈrēbrəl, ˈserəbrəl

deplete
diˈplēt

extemporize
ikˈstempəˌrīz

humane
(h)yoōˈmān

Christian was an avid fan of many genres of film, but he particularly fancied **cerebral** movies that made him think deeply about certain issues or that delve into the psychology of a character. For example, he absolutely loved *American Psycho* (2000), a film about an investment banker with an ostentatious and shallow lifestyle who hides his psychopathic ego and **libertine** fantasies from his co-workers and friends. As the movie progresses, he begins to escalate deeper into his fantasies, and his actions become less and less **humane**. He begins going on a murdering rampage and kills many people, including his co-worker (in a scene which was heavily **extemporized**.) By the end of the film, the character's sanity seems to be completely **depleted**, and the audience is left unsure of what is real and what is not.

Definitions: Try matching the words in the list with the appropriate definitions. If you are stuck, check the glossary in the back of the book or the passage at the top of the page.

1.	libertine	_____	a.	to use up the supply or resources of
2.	cerebral	_____	b.	having or showing compassion or benevolence
3.	deplete	_____	c.	intellectual and not emotional
4.	extemporize	_____	d.	characterized by a disregard for morality
5.	humane	_____	e.	to improvise; to create and perform spontaneously and without preparation

Sentences: Try to use the words above in a sentence below. Remember that a word ending may be changed or its figure of speech slightly altered.

6. Clyde prefers to read _____ novels that make him think about important philosophical questions.

7. Miles often did not prepare much for his jazz performances, choosing to _____ a majority of the time that he was on stage.

8. If we are not mindful of the way we use the Earth's resources, they may be _____ sooner than we expect.

9. Stacy's veterinary clinic was respected for its _____ methods of euthanizing sick animals.

10. Kevin's willingness to indulge himself at the expense of others was indicative of his _____ attitude.

Lesson 168

TEAMWORK MAKES THE DREAM WORK

Jenna and Helga were working together to create a **diorama** of the solar system for their science class. Jenna had hoped to make the project intricate and **dynamic** with many moving parts to demonstrate the rotation and revolution of the planets, but the project was due the next day and the girls had barely even begun! The girls did not make a very effective team — Jenna tended to be **domineering**, ordering Helga to complete tasks without consulting her first, whereas Helga was quite lazy. She refused to put in any actual effort because, in her **odious** attitude, she believed that if they were meant to get a good grade on the project, they would get it regardless of how much work they put into it. Their lack of teamwork was the biggest **obstruction** to their productivity, and they ended up receiving a failing grade for their shoddy project.

Definitions: Try matching the words in the list with the appropriate definitions. If you are stuck, check the glossary in the back of the book or the passage at the top of the page.

1.	odious	_____	a.	a thing that impedes or prevents passage or progress
2.	diorama	_____	b.	overly controlling
3.	dynamic	_____	c.	a three-dimensional model of a scene
4.	obstruction	_____	d.	extremely unpleasant
5.	domineering	_____	e.	always changing or active

Sentences: Try to use the words above in a sentence below. Remember that a word ending may be changed or its figure of speech slightly altered.

6.   It would be _____ to invite the thieves who robbed your best friend's home over for coffee in your living room.

7.   One of the reasons why Albert decided to quit was because of his boss's _____ personality, which made it difficult to enjoy work.

8.   After the hurricane, many of the homeowners in the neighborhood worked together to clear fallen trees and other _____ from the road.

9.   Ralph decided to create a realistic _____ of a scene from his favorite book for his art project.

10.   Due to the _____ work environment, there was never a dull moment at the office.

NEW WORDS

resignation
ˌrezigˈnāSHən

foresight
ˈfôrˌsīt

elongated
iˈlôNGˌgātid, iˈläNG-

havoc
ˈhavək

tacit
ˈtasit

With much **resignation**, Brandon, a former lieutenant in the Baltimore police department, accepted the fact that he was going to be dismissed. He did not want to give up his position, but he did not have much of a choice. He had recently been involved in a drunk driving accident, which had caused much **havoc** at a busy intersection. Brandon wished that he had had the **foresight** to see the consequences of his bad decision, but this was not the case. After word got out that he had been the cause of the accident, the chief of police made the **tacit** suggestion that Brandon should take responsibility for his actions and resign rather than force the department to fire him directly. Brandon reluctantly agreed, displaying an **elongated** frown and a tear in his eye.

Definitions: Try matching the words in the list with the appropriate definitions. If you are stuck, check the glossary in the back of the book or the passage at the top of the page.

1.	resignation	_____	a.	the ability to predict what will happen in the future
2.	foresight	_____	b.	understood or implied without being stated
3.	elongated	_____	c.	widespread destruction, confusion, or disorder
4.	havoc	_____	d.	unusually long in relation to its width
5.	tacit	_____	e.	1. an act of retiring or giving up a position; 2. the acceptance of something undesirable but inevitable

Sentences: Try to use the words above in a sentence below. Remember that a word ending may be changed or its figure of speech slightly altered.

6. If John had not had the _____ to bring his raincoat, he would have gotten drenched during the sudden downpour.

7. The house fire caused much _____ within the normally peaceful neighborhood.

8. Bruce met the fact that he was going to be fired with _____: there was nothing he could do to prevent being dismissed.

9. A lack of response will be regarded as a(n) _____ agreement.

10. The _____ necks of giraffes allow them to eat leaves on high branches almost effortlessly.

NEW WORDS

dissolute
ˈdisəˌlo͞ot

stark
stärk

ameliorate
əˈmēlyəˌrāt, əˈmēlēə-

fortify
ˈfôrtəˌfī

terse
tərs

MARRIAGE TROUBLES

Sally had started to become worried about her husband's behavior. Over the past couple of months, Harry had begun to lead a more **dissolute** lifestyle and would often come home after work quite intoxicated. He had also seemed to become more emotionally distant from Sally, giving **terse** responses to her questions and sometimes ignoring her altogether. This was in **stark** contrast to the way he used be – full of energy, enthusiasm, and a zeal for life that had drawn Sally to him in the first place. Harry's progressively worsening behavior prompted Sally to seek the help of a marriage counselor to try and **fortify** their relationship, hoping to **ameliorate** the situation before it became unsalvageable.

Definitions: Try matching the words in the list with the appropriate definitions. If you are stuck, check the glossary in the back of the book or the passage at the top of the page.

1.	dissolute	_____	a.	to strengthen
2.	stark	_____	b.	brief and direct in a way that may seem unfriendly
3.	ameliorate	_____	c.	severe or bare in appearance; sharply clear
4.	fortify	_____	d.	lax in morals
5.	terse	_____	e.	to make something bad, unfortunate, or unsatisfactory better

Sentences: Try to use the words above in a sentence below. Remember that a word ending may be changed or its figure of speech slightly altered.

6.   Although they were siblings, there was a(n) _____ difference in the way the two brothers behaved.

7.   The workers _____ the house with extra support to protect it from severe weather.

8.   It was difficult to have a conversation with Richard, who was an unusually quiet person that often responded in a(n) _____ manner.

9.   The drunken man often offended others with his _____ actions.

10.   Jerry volunteered much of his time to the local orphanage in hopes of _____ the unfortunate situations of the children there.

Crossword Puzzle
Lessons 161-170

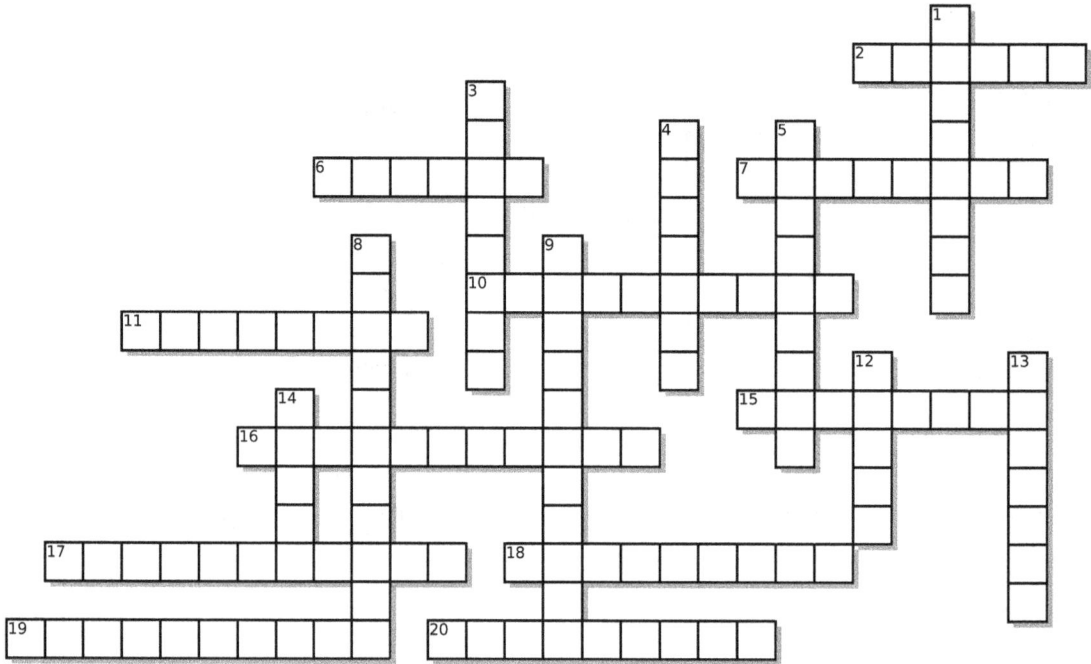

ACROSS

2 lacking sophistication or good taste
6 1. a state of extravagant living; 2. an inessential desirable item that is expensive
7 to knock or force out of position
10 to make something bad, unfortunate, or unsatisfactory better
11 to make less severe or unpleasant without removing the cause
15 relating to the sense of hearing
16 a state of low spirits due to loss of hope or courage
17 overly controlling
18 characterized by a disregard for morality
19 1. a great disaster; 2. the end of the world
20 unusually long in relation to its width

DOWN

1 to coax with kind words or flattery
3 1. property that is inherited; 2. objects or traditions, values, historical buildings or countryside passed down from previous generations
4 extremely passionate about or devoted to (sometimes in a negative way)
5 morally right or justifiable
8 to improvise; to create and perform spontaneously and without preparation
9 1. an act of retiring or giving up a position; 2. the acceptance of something undesirable but inevitable
12 unable to bend or be forced out of shape
13 always changing or active
14 brief and direct in a way that may seem unfriendly

Vocabulary Review
Lessons 161-170

Directions: Match each word with its best approximate definition. Note that definitions are not necessarily repeated verbatim from the lesson exercises.

1.	morass	_____	a.	disappointed by someone or something that was previously esteemed
2.	adamant	_____	b.	distress and/or embarrassment for having failed or been humiliate
3.	chagrin	_____	c.	to increase the power, wealth, status, or reputation of
4.	jingoism	_____	d.	intellectual (as opposed to emotional or physical)
5.	stimulate	_____	e.	a boggy or swampy area; a difficult or complicated situation
6.	tenet	_____	f.	widespread destruction; great confusion or disorder
7.	disenchanted	_____	g.	playful and often troublemaking misbehavior, especially in children
8.	noxious	_____	h.	severe in appearance; complete
9.	aggrandize	_____	i.	extremely unpleasant; repulsive
10.	precede	_____	j.	harmful, poisonous, or very unpleasant
11.	mischief	_____	k.	implied or understood without being stated
12.	amorphous	_____	l.	a model representing a scene with three dimensional figures
13.	cerebral	_____	m.	a key principle or belief
14.	humane	_____	n.	to come before or ahead of another in time or position
15.	odious	_____	o.	to make someone or something more active or excited
16.	diorama	_____	p.	to strengthen physically or mentally
17.	havoc	_____	q.	refusing to be persuaded to change one's mind
18.	tacit	_____	r.	showing kindness and compassion
19.	stark	_____	s.	lacking a clearly defined shape or form
20.	fortify	_____	t.	extreme and hostile patriotism

Literary and Drama Terms

Whether you have a passion for literature or you feel forced to learn it for exams, there are terms that you should know. Below is a list of major literary terms that will help you better understand how literature operates.

alliteration: the use of the same letter or sound at the beginning of adjacent or nearly connected words

analogy: a comparison between two things, usually for the purpose of instruction or clarification

anecdote: a short, catchy story about an intriguing incident or person

eulogy: a speech or writing that praises someone excessively, often after that person's death

foreshadow: something that serves as a warning or indication of a future event

hyperbole: claims or statements that are so exaggerated as to not be able to be taken literally in a serious manner

irony: a set of affairs or circumstances that seems to be the exact opposite of what one would expect, thus resulting in amusement

foil (n.): a character or object used for contrast in order to emphasize and enhance the qualities of another

metaphor:	a figure of speech where a word or phrase is applied to an action to which it cannot in reality or literally be applied; a thing that is regarded as symbolic or representative of something else
onomatopoeia:	the use of a word that sounds exactly like its name (e.g. ding dong, boom, cuckoo)
personification:	the attribution of human characteristics to something that is nonhuman; giving some abstract entity humanlike attributes
plot:	the main events of a novel, play, or other work presented in some form of sequence
pseudonym:	a fictitious name used by an author of a work, almost always because the author does not want to reveal his or her identity
setting:	the place and time in which a novel, short story, play, or other event takes place
simile:	a figure of speech comparing one thing with another using "like" or "as" in the comparison
soliloquy:	often used in a play, the act of speaking or reading one's feelings aloud – regardless of whether other people are present
synopsis:	a brief summary of a piece of writing, drama, film, or other piece of art

ANSWER KEY

Lesson 121

1. b
2. a
3. e
4. c
5. d
6. perturbed
7. winnow
8. multifaceted
9. rudimentary
10. elicited

Lesson 122

1. d
2. a
3. b
4. e
5. c
6. waxing
7. desecration
8. inception
9. cloying
10. procrastinating

Lesson 123

1. e
2. a
3. c
4. b
5. d
6. reclusive
7. dithering
8. vicarious
9. dumbfounded
10. pruned

Lesson 124

1. d
2. a
3. e
4. c
5. b
6. delinquent
7. sarcastic
8. viable
9. miscalculation
10. enhance

Lesson 125

1. c
2. a
3. e
4. b
5. d
6. waned
7. expropriated
8. detonating
9. pithy
10. lighthearted

Lesson 126

1. b
2. a
3. d
4. e
5. c
6. menace
7. diverge
8. potable
9. apprise
10. illicit

Lesson 127

1. b
2. e
3. a
4. c
5. d
6. reparations
7. ingenious
8. equivocate
9. foibles
10. venerated

Lesson 128

1. c
2. a
3. b
4. e
5. d
6. demure
7. spur
8. hypocritical
9. unadorned
10. fetid

Lesson 129

1. c
2. b
3. d
4. e
5. a
6. benefactors
7. impoverished
8. reserve
9. proclivity
10. averting

Lesson 130

1. b
2. a
3. d
4. e
5. c
6. ostracized

7. sedulous
8. receptacle
9. malaise
10. mischance

Crossword Puzzle: Lessons 121-130

Review: Lessons 121-130

1. c
2. q
3. s
4. a
5. n
6. j
7. b
8. g
9. h
10. t
11. e
12. f
13. o
14. i
15. k
16. d
17. l
18. p
19. r
20. m

Lesson 131

1. c
2. d
3. e
4. a
5. b
6. stereotyped
7. grandeur
8. expeditiously
9. coddle
10. truce

Lesson 132

1. c
2. e
3. d
4. b
5. a
6. canvas
7. dilemma
8. gargantuan
9. animate
10. lax

Lesson 133

1. b
2. a
3. e
4. c
5. d
6. outdated
7. abstain
8. overt
9. tangent
10. fallacious

Lesson 134

1. b
2. c
3. e
4. d
5. a
6. posthumously
7. stoic
8. acquiesce
9. misanthrope
10. synopsis

Lesson 135

1. b
2. c
3. a
4. e
5. d
6. persevered
7. precipice
8. unanimous
9. conjoined
10. talisman

Lesson 136

1. e
2. c
3. d
4. a
5. b
6. affluent
7. convergence
8. ambition
9. discerning
10. transgression

Lesson 137

1. b
2. d
3. e
4. c
5. a
6. jaded
7. stymied
8. detractor
9. concession
10. formulate

Lesson 138

1. d
2. c
3. e
4. a
5. b
6. summon
7. compilation
8. impressionistic
9. swarthy
10. torpid

Lesson 139

1. b
2. a
3. e
4. c
5. d
6. vivid
7. mandatory
8. despair
9. winced
10. disputation

Lesson 140

1. a
2. c
3. b
4. e
5. d
6. affable
7. haphazardly
8. mustered
9. obdurate
10. recessive

Word Search: Lessons 131-140

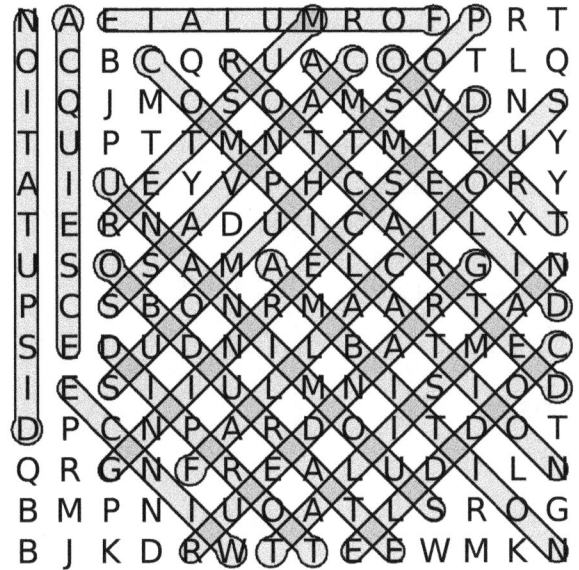

Review: Lessons 131-140

1. j
2. q
3. b
4. o
5. t
6. g
7. i
8. r
9. a
10. d
11. c
12. m
13. k
14. s
15. l
16. n
17. p
18. h
19. f
20. e

Lesson 141

1. c
2. d
3. b
4. e
5. a
6. deluged
7. blare
8. melodramatic
9. panorama
10. rigorous

Lesson 142

1. e
2. c
3. a
4. b
5. d
6. placate
7. scintillating
8. slovenly
9. prophetic
10. conjure

Lesson 143

1. a
2. e
3. b
4. c
5. d
6. preponderance
7. culpable
8. dissipate
9. subversive
10. abject

Lesson 144

1. a
2. c
3. d
4. b
5. e
6. obstinate
7. enrage
8. denotation
9. obtrusively
10. manorial

Lesson 145

1. a
2. c
3. b
4. e
5. d
6. connotation
7. refined
8. espouse
9. penitent
10. knell

Lesson 146

1. c
2. a
3. e
4. b
5. d
6. outspoken
7. contingency
8. presentiment
9. plague
10. disjointed

Lesson 147

1. b
2. a
3. e
4. d
5. c
6. seduce
7. dispassionate
8. temperate
9. remiss
10. brouhaha

Lesson 148

1. b
2. e
3. d
4. a
5. c
6. prophecies
7. grandiloquent
8. catalyst
9. marshal
10. suffrage

Lesson 149

1. a
2. c
3. d
4. e
5. b
6. archipelago
7. rousing
8. anthropological
9. complicity
10. exacting

Lesson 150

1. a
2. c
3. d
4. e
5. b
6. progressive
7. surpasses
8. irksome
9. peevish
10. propitious

Crossword Puzzle: Lessons 141-150

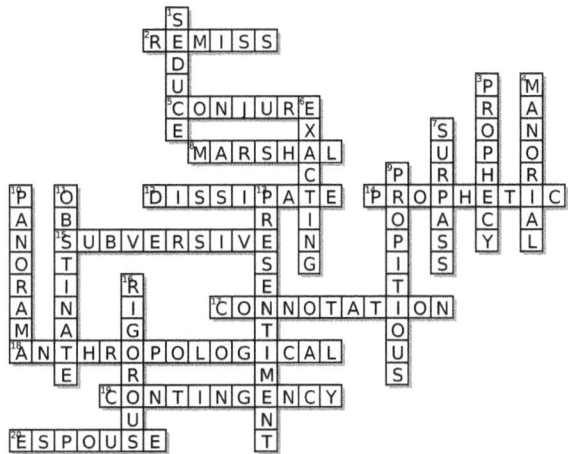

Review: Lessons 141-150

1. j
2. b
3. t
4. q
5. l
6. o
7. d
8. s
9. c
10. g
11. f
12. n
13. a
14. h
15. p
16. m
17. r
18. i
19. k
20. e

Lesson 151

1. b
2. a
3. d
4. e
5. c

6. bemoaning
7. pernicious
8. lackadaisical
9. intrusion
10. pluralism

Lesson 152

1. b
2. a
3. d
4. e
5. c
6. stringent
7. decorous
8. pliable
9. vaccines
10. yen

Lesson 153

1. c
2. e
3. a
4. b
5. d
6. prestigious
7. slipshod
8. immense
9. organic
10. maneuvering

Lesson 154

1. c
2. d
3. a
4. e
5. b
6. laborious
7. hedonistic
8. adhere
9. spate
10. averse

Lesson 155

1. b
2. e
3. a
4. c
5. d
6. tedious
7. succulent
8. unhinged
9. provincial
10. presumptive

Lesson 156

1. b
2. e
3. a
4. c
5. d
6. alienated
7. disparity
8. exempt
9. audacity
10. factions

Lesson 157

1. e
2. b
3. d
4. a
5. c
6. elucidate
7. mediation
8. segregation
9. parched
10. turpitude

Lesson 158

1. b
2. a
3. d
4. e
5. c

6. acoustic
7. escalated
8. impecunious
9. plunged
10. doctrinaire

Lesson 159

1. a
2. d
3. c
4. e
5. b
6. holistic
7. intrinsic
8. perpetual
9. transitory
10. mirth

Lesson 160

1. a
2. e
3. d
4. c
5. b
6. linchpin
7. incidental
8. fouled
9. surmounted
10. commended

Word Search: Lessons 151-160

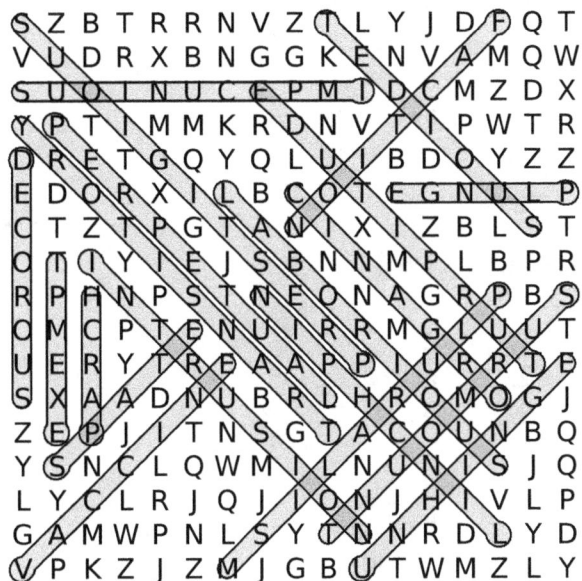

Review: Lessons 151-160

1. k
2. a
3. p
4. b
5. r
6. o
7. f
8. d
9. t
10. n
11. m
12. h
13. g
14. q
15. i
16. c
17. j
18. l
19. e
20. s

Lesson 161

1. c
2. d

3.   a
4.   e
5.   b
6.   adamant
7.   refract
8.   morass
9.   auditory
10. righteous

Lesson 162

1.   c
2.   a
3.   e
4.   b
5.   d
6.   heritage
7.   dislodge
8.   chagrin
9.   figurative
10. jingoism

Lesson 163

1.   d
2.   e
3.   a
4.   c
5.   b
6.   rigid
7.   predilection
8.   palliating
9.   tenets
10. stimulated

Lesson 164

1.   e
2.   d
3.   a
4.   c
5.   b
6.   blandish
7.   disenchanted
8.   noxious
9.   despondence
10. appraising

Lesson 165

1.   c
2.   d
3.   a
4.   e
5.   b
6.   vulgar
7.   decisive
8.   preceded
9.   luxury
10. aggrandize

Lesson 166

1.   b
2.   d
3.   a
4.   e
5.   c
6.   mischief
7.   amorphous
8.   apocalypse
9.   zealous
10. invasive

Lesson 167

1.   d
2.   c
3.   a
4.   e
5.   b
6.   cerebral
7.   extemporize
8.   depleted
9.   humane
10. libertine

Lesson 168

1.   d
2.   c
3.   e
4.   a
5.   b

6. odious
7. domineering
8. obstructions
9. diorama
10. dynamic

Lesson 169

1. e
2. a
3. d
4. c
5. b
6. foresight
7. havoc
8. resignation
9. tacit
10. elongated

Lesson 170

1. d
2. c
3. e
4. a
5. b
6. stark
7. fortified
8. terse
9. dissolute
10. ameliorating

Crossword Puzzle: Lessons 161-170

Review: Lessons 161-170

1. e
2. q
3. b
4. t
5. o
6. m
7. a
8. j
9. c
10. n
11. g
12. s
13. d
14. r
15. i
16. l
17. f
18. k
19. h
20. p

GLOSSARY

This glossary contains definitions of the new words from every lesson contained in this book. Please note that not every meaning of each word is contained in this glossary. Generally, only the most commonly used meanings of the words below are defined.

All entries in the glossary take the following form:

word (lesson): (part of speech) definition

Key for parts of speech:
adj. = adjective   adv. = adverb   n. = noun   v. = verb

A

abject (143): (adj.) extremely miserable and unfortunate; contemptible, self-abashing

abstain (133): (v.) to resist doing something or to resist being tempted by something

acoustic (158): (adj.) relating to sound, hearing

acquiesce (134): (v.) to agree or give in

adamant (161): (adj.) refusing to be persuaded

adhere (154): (v.) to stick to firmly; to follow through

affable (140): (adj.) friendly, cordial

affluence (136): (n.) great wealth

aggrandize (165): (v.) to make great or greater

alienate (156): (v.) to make someone feel isolated or estranged

ambition (136): (n.) a strong desire to succeed

ameliorate (170): (v.) to make something bad, unfortunate, or unsatisfactory better

amorphous (166): (adj.) without clearly defined shape or form

animate (132): (adj.) alive or having life; (v.) 1. to bring to life or enliven; 2. to give renewed inspiration or encouragement to something

anthropological (149): (adj.) relating to the study of humankind

apocalypse (166): (n.) 1. a great disaster; 2. the end of the world

appraise (164): (v.) to assess the value or quality of

apprise (126): (v.) to inform or advise

archipelago (149): (n.) a group of islands oneself in speech or writing clearly and/or persuasively

audacious (156): (adj.) bold, daring

auditory (161): (adj.) relating to the sense of hearing

averse (154): (adj.) strongly opposed to

avert (129): (v.) to prevent or ward off an undesirable occurrence

B

bemoan (151): (v.) to lament; to grieve

benefactors (129): (n.) people who give money or other help to a person or a cause

blandish (164): (v.) to coax with kind words or flattery

blare (141): (v.) to make a loud, harsh noise

brouhaha (147): (n.) excited public response to something

C

canvass (132): (v.) 1. to try to obtain or request something, especially votes from people; 2. to try to get someone's opinion; 3. to discuss thoroughly

catalyst (148): (n.) stimulus to make change happen

cerebral (167): (adj.) intellectual and not emotional

chagrin (162): (n.) distress or embarrassment at having failed or been humiliated

cloying (122): (adj.) displeasing because of excess of sweetness or richness or sentiment

coddle (131): (v.) to treat with excessive indulgence

commend (160): (v.) to praise; to endorse

compilation (138): (n.) a process or act of assembling different sources to put together something; something that is compiled

complicity (149): (n.) involvement with others in a crime or something illegal

concession (137): (n.) something granted in response to demands; a preferential allowance given by an organization or government

conjoin (135): (v.) to connect, to join

conjure (142): (v.) to gather, to bring something into existence

connotation (145): (n.) an idea or feeling that is implied or evoked by a term

contingency (146): (n.) a possible event that might happen in the future; a provision for an unforeseen circumstance

convergence (136): (n.) the act of coming together

culpable (143): (adj.) to be guilty and blameworthy for

D

decisive (165): (adj.) able to make choices quickly and/or confidently

decorous (152): (adj.) keeping with good propriety and taste; polite and restrained

delinquent (124): (adj.) 1. showing a tendency to commit a crime, especially youth; 2. irresponsible; 3. in arrears; (n.) a youth likely to commit a crime

deluge (141): (n.) a large amount of something coming at the same time; (v.) to flood with something

demure (128): (adj.) reserved, modest, and shy

denotation (144): (n.) indication of something using words, symbols; the primary meaning of a word

deplete (167): (v.) to use up the supply or resources of

desecration (122): (n.) blasphemy; violation

despair (139): (n.) hopelessness, pessimism

despondence (164): (n.) a state of low spirits due to loss of hope or courage

detonate (125): (v.) to explode; to burst

detractor (137): (n.) a person who criticizes or belittles the value of something

dilemma (132): (n.) a difficult situation requiring a choice between two or more equally unfavorable options

diorama (168): (n.) a three-dimensional model of a scene

discerning (136): (adj.) perceptive, having good judgment; able to detect great subtlety

disenchanted (164): (adj.) disappointed by someone or something previously respected or admired

disjointed (146): (adj.) divided, lacking continuity or organization

dislodge (162): (v.) to knock or force out of position

disparity (156): (n.) a great difference between things

dispassionate (147): (adj.) uninfluenced by strong emotions

disputation (139): (n.) debate or argument

dissipate (143): (v.) to disperse; to waste away

dissolute (170): (adj.) lax in morals

dither (123): (v.) to be indecisive

diverge (126): (v.) to separate from a path or route and go in a different direction

doctrinaire (158): (adj.) insistent on using theory or doctrine without considering practicality

domineering (168): (adj.) overly controlling

dumbfounded (123): (adj.) astounded; bewildered

dynamic (168): (adj.) always changing or active

E

elicit (121): (v.) to evoke; to draw out

elongated (169): (adj.) unusually long in relation to its width

elucidate (157): (v.) to clarify; to illuminate

enhance (124): (v.) to intensify, increase, or improve the extent, quality, or value thereof

enrage (144): (v.) to make angry

equivocate (127): (v.) to use ambiguous language to avoid commitment or to hide the truth

escalate (158): (v.) to become more serious and intense

espouse (145): (v.) to adopt and promote a cause, theory, or belief

exacting (149): (adj.) demanding great attention to detail

exempt (156): (adj.) free from liability or obligation imposed on others; (n.) a person who is free of liability for something, usually paying tax; (v.) to free a person from an obligation or liability imposed on others

expeditious (131): (adj.) being quick and still ensuring good result

expropriate (125): (v.) (usually of a government) to seize and take away (usually property) from its owner

extemporize (167): (v.) to improvise; to create and perform spontaneously and without preparation

F

faction (156): (n.) a small dissenting group within a larger group, especially in politics

fallacious (133): (adj.) something based on a mistaken belief

fetid (128): (adj.) smelling extremely unpleasant

figurative (162): (adj.) metaphorical, not literal

foible (127): (n.) a minor weakness, defect, or eccentricity in someone's behavior

foresight (169): (n.) the ability to predict what will happen in the future

formulate (137): (v.) to create methodically; articulate, express

fortify (170): (v.) to strengthen

fouled (160): (v.) made dirty, defiled, or soiled

G

gargantuan (132): (adj.) of great quantity; huge, giant

grandeur (131): (n.) quality of being impressive or splendid in style

grandiloquent (148): (adj.) pompous in style or manner; designed in a way to impress

H

haphazard (140): (adj.) unplanned, lacking organization

havoc (169): (n.) widespread destruction, confusion, or disorder

hedonistic (154): (adj.) seeking pleasure, especially for self- indulgence

heritage (162): (n.) 1. property that is inherited; 2. objects or traditions, values, historical buildings or countryside passed down from previous generations

holistic (159): (adj.) considering all factors, all-inclusive

humane (167): (adj.) having or showing compassion or benevolence

hypocritical (128): (adj.) behaving in a way that indicates someone has higher moral standards than is reality

I

illicit (126): (adj.) illegal; prohibited

immense (153): (adj.) extremely strong, in great quantity

impecunious (158): (adj.) having little or no money

impoverish (129): (v.) to exhaust; to reduce to poverty

impressionistic (138): (adj.) based on unsystematic, subjective reactions

inception (122): (n.) beginning; initiation

incidental (160): (adj.) occurring as a consequence; secondary, subordinate

ingenious (127): (adj.) clever; brilliant

intrinsic (159): (adj.) inherent, innate, essential

intrusion (151): (n.) unwelcome entrance which disturbs; something unwelcome

invasive (166): (adj.) tending to spread undesirably or harmfully

irksome (150): (adj.) annoying in a tiresome way

J

jaded (137): (adj.) tired, lacking enthusiasm, or bored, usually after having too much of something

jingoism (162): (n.) extreme patriotism

K

knell (145): (n.) the sound of a bell, usually in reference to the dead or a funeral

L

laborious (154): (adj.) arduous, demanding great effort and time

lackadaisical (151): (adj.) lacking enthusiasm or effort

lax (132): (adj.) slipshod, not sufficiently strict or careful

libertine (167): (adj.) characterized by a disregard for morality

lighthearted (125): (adj.) carefree; jovial

linchpin (160): (n.) a person or thing vital to a business or an organization

luxury (165): (n.) 1. a state of extravagant living; 2. an inessential desirable item that is expensive

M

malaise (130): (n.) depression, anxiety

mandatory (139): (adj.) required by rule, compulsory

maneuver (153): (n.) 1. a movement or series of movements requiring care and skill; 2. a carefully planned scheme often using deception; (v.) 1. to manipulate; 2. to turn or move skillfully

manorial (144): (adj.) of or pertaining to a large country house with lands or the principal home of a landed estate (often in medieval times)

marshal (148): (n.) 1. an officer of the highest rank in the armed forces in certain countries; 2. a municipal officer or head of a police department; 3. an official responsible for supervising public events; (v.) to arrange or assemble in order

mediation (157): (n.) act of intervention to resolve conflicts

melodramatic (141): (adj.) exaggerated and overemotional

menace (126): (n.) 1. a danger or threat; 2. a person or thing causing a danger or threat; (v.) to threaten in a hostile manner

mirth (159): (n.) amusement – often expressed by laughter

misanthrope (134): (n.) one who dislikes people in general

miscalculate (124): (v.) 1. to assess a situation wrongly; 2. to measure an amount, distance, or value wrongly

mischance (130): (n.) bad luck

mischief (166): (n.) playful misbehavior or troublemaking

morass (161): (n.) 1. an area of boggy ground; 2. a complicated or confusing situation

multifaceted (121): (adj.) versatile; having many aspects

muster (140): (v.) to assemble a group of people; to call up (a) feeling(s), emotion(s), or response(s)

N

noxious (164): (adj.) harmful; poisonous; extremely unpleasant

O

obdurate (140): (adj.) stubborn, resistant to change

obstinate (144): (adj.) stubbornly persistent, unwilling to yield

obstruction (168): (n.) a thing that impedes or prevents passage or progress

obtrusive (144): (adj.) noticeable or prominent in an unwelcome manner

odious (168): (adj.) extremely unpleasant

organic (153): (adj.) 1. relating to living things; 2. produced without the use of chemical agents; 3. constitutional, essential as parts of a whole

ostracize (130): (v.) to exclude someone from a group

outdated (133): (adj.) obsolete; no longer in trend

outspoken (146): (adj.) expressing one's opinion freely and frankly

overt (133): (adj.) done or shown openly; readily apparent

P

palliate (163): (v.) to make less severe or unpleasant without removing the cause

panorama (141): (n.) a wide, continuous view; an overall picture or thorough survey of something

parch (157): (v.) to dry something completely through heat

peevish (150): (adj.) bad-tempered, tending to complain

penitent (145): (adj.) repentant, regretful

pernicious (151): (adj.) causing great harm, malicious

perpetual (159): (adj.) occurring repeatedly; lasting forever

persevere (135): (v.) to persist, to refuse to stop despite obstacles

perturbed (121): (adj.) troubled; perplexed

pithy (125): (adj.) concise and strongly expressive

placate (142): (v.) to calm, soothe, appease

plague (146): (n.) a thing or person that causes trouble and unhappiness; (v.) to cause distress

pliable (152): (adj.) flexible, easily bent or molded

plunge (158): (n.) a jump or dive into water; 2. a swift and drastic fall in value or amount; (v.) 1. to move downward or drop steeply; 2. to embark on something with vigor

pluralism (151): (n.) co-existence of groups of different backgrounds within one society

posthumous (134): (adj.) happening after a person's death

potable (126): (adj.) something safe to drink; drinkable

precede (165): (v.) to happen or come before (in time)

precipice (135): (n.) a very tall and steep cliff (literal or figurative)

predilection (163): (n.) a preference or special liking for something

preponderance (143): (n.) being greater in number, importance, or quantity

presentiment (146): (n.) a gut feeling about the future, likely one of a foreboding nature

prestigious (153): (adj.) having great reputation

presumptive (155): (adj.) taking something to be true or adopting a particular attitude toward something

proclivity (129): (n.) tendency; inclination

procrastinate (122): (v.) to delay or put off

progressive (150): (adj.) advancing gradually

prophecy (148): (n.) prediction of future event

prophetic (142): (adj.) accurately predictive of the future

propitious (150): (adj.) favorable; likely to result in success

provincial (155): (adj.) narrow-minded, unsophisticated

prune (123): (n.) a plum preserved by drying out; (v.) to trim; to remove the superfluous elements

R

receptacle (130): (n.) container; a place for holding or storing

recessive (140): (adj.) genetic trait that is exhibited only when inherited from both parents

reclusive (123): (adj.) unsociable; solitary

refined (145): (adj.) cultivated in manner, appearance, taste; free from impurities

refract (161): (v.) to make a ray of light change direction when it enters a medium at an angle

remiss (147): (adj.) negligent, careless in one's duty

reparation (127): (n.) restitution; making amends; paying money to those who have been wronged

reserve (129): (v.) to hold for future use

resignation (169): (n.) 1. an act of retiring or giving up a position; 2. the acceptance of something undesirable but inevitable

righteous (161): (adj.) morally right or justifiable

rigid (163): (adj.) unable to bend or be forced out of shape

rigorous (141): (adj.) painstaking and exact; demanding, harsh

rousing (149): (adj.) inciting enthusiasm, full of energy

rudimentary (121): (adj.) basic; elementary

S

sarcastic (124): (adj.) speech using irony in order to mock or to show contempt

scintillating (142): (adj.) shining brightly; clever and brilliant

seduce (147): (v.) to lure someone into inadvisable courses of action or beliefs

sedulous (130): (adj.) assiduous; diligent

segregation (157): (n.) separation into groups

slipshod (153): (adj.) done in a careless manner

slovenly (142): (adj.) ill-groomed and untidy; careless, negligent

spate (154): (n.) a large number or amount of something happening in quick succession

spur (128): (v.) to incite or stimulate

stark (170): (adj.) severe or bare in appearance; sharply clear

stereotype (131): (n.) commonly held idea or image about a specific group of people; (v.) treat with preconceived notion

stimulate (163): (v.) to make (something) more active or excited

stoic (134): (adj.) calm, seemingly emotionless

stringent (152): (adj.) rigorous, strictly controlled

stymie (137): (v.) to hinder the progress of

subversive (143): (adj.) attempting to undermine an established system; (n.) a revolutionist, insurgent

succulent (155): (adj.) juicy and tasty

suffrage (148): (n.) the right to vote

summon (138): (v.) 1. to authoritatively or urgently call on someone or something to be present; 2. to call people to attend a meeting; 3. to urgently demand help; 4. to bring to the surface a quality or reaction from within oneself

surmount (160): (v.) to overcome; to get over something

surpass (150): (v.) go beyond expectation

swarthy (138): (adj.) dark-skinned

synopsis (134): (n.) a brief summary or outline of a text

T

tacit (169): (adj.) understood or implied without being stated

talisman (135): (n.) an object (usually a stone, ring, or necklace) thought to possess magical powers

tangent (133): (n.) a digression from the main topic

tedious (155): (adj.) boring and tiresome due to dull repetition

temperate (147): (adj.) moderate; restrained in one's behavior

tenet (163): (n.) a principle or belief

terse (170): (adj.) brief and direct in a way that may seem unfriendly

torpid (138): (adj.) mentally or physically inactive; sluggish

transgression (136): (n.) an act that violates a rule, law, or principle; an offense

transitory (159): (adj.) fleeting, not lasting

truce (131): (n.) an agreement between opponents to end their conflicts and discuss peace terms

turpitude (157): (n.) depravity; wickedness

U

unadorned (128): (adj.) plain and simple, undecorated

unanimous (135): (adj.) two or more people in complete agreement, held by everyone involved

unhinge (155): (v.) 1. to make someone mentally unbalanced; 2. to deprive of stability or fixity; 3. to take a door off its hinges

V

vaccine (152): (n.) substance used to provide immunity against certain diseases; protective software

venerate (127): (v.) to revere; to idolize

viable (124): (adj.) applicable; feasible

vicarious (123): (adj.) experienced in the imagination through the actions or feelings of another individual

vivid (139): (adj.) suggesting a clear and lively image; evoking strong feeling; intense in color

vulgar (165): (adj.) lacking sophistication or good taste

W

wane (125): (v.) to diminish or lessen

wax (122): (v.) to become larger

wince (139): (n.) a facial or bodily response to suggest pain, distress; (v.) to recoil, draw back due to pain or fear

winnow (121): (v.) to distinguish; to sift out; to separate out

Y

yen (152): (n.) a strong yearning for something; (v.) to yearn for something

Z

zealous (166): (adj.) extremely passionate about or devoted to sometimes in a negative way

www.ingramcontent.com/pod-product-compliance
Lightning Source LLC
Chambersburg PA
CBHW081538040426
42447CB00014B/3422